# BIRD WATCHING

## Log Book

*This Book Belongs To*

Name: ................................................

Phone: ................................................

Email:

## PHOTO / SKETCH

## HEAD

| | |
|---|---|
| SPECIES | |
| SEX / AGE | |
| BEHAVIOR | |
| VOICE | |
| BODY | |
| LEGS / FEET | |
| HABITAT | |

## LOCATION

LOCATION NAME

GPS COORDINATES

## MONTH SPOTTED

| J | F | M | A | M | J | J | A | S | O | N | D |
|---|---|---|---|---|---|---|---|---|---|---|---|

## ADDITIONAL NOTES

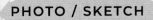

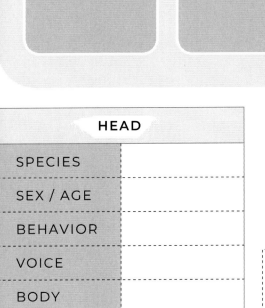

## HEAD

| SPECIES | |
|---|---|
| SEX / AGE | |
| BEHAVIOR | |
| VOICE | |
| BODY | |
| LEGS / FEET | |
| HABITAT | |

## LOCATION

LOCATION NAME

GPS COORDINATES

— ◌ ◌ ◌ ◌ ◌

— ◌ ◌ ◌ ◌ ◌

## MONTH SPOTTED

| J | F | M | A | M | J | J | A | S | O | N | D |
|---|---|---|---|---|---|---|---|---|---|---|---|

## ADDITIONAL NOTES

## PHOTO / SKETCH

## HEAD

| | |
|---|---|
| SPECIES | |
| SEX / AGE | |
| BEHAVIOR | |
| VOICE | |
| BODY | |
| LEGS / FEET | |
| HABITAT | |

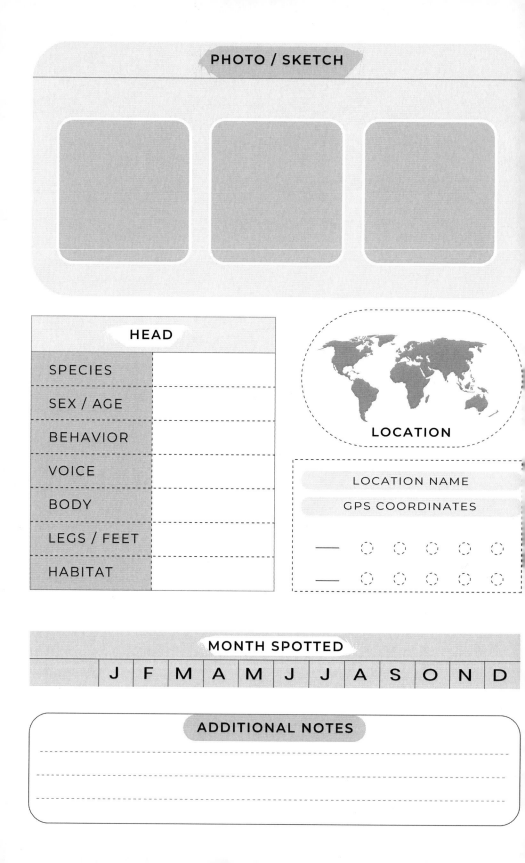

## LOCATION

LOCATION NAME

GPS COORDINATES

—  ◌ ◌ ◌ ◌ ◌

—  ◌ ◌ ◌ ◌ ◌

## MONTH SPOTTED

| J | F | M | A | M | J | J | A | S | O | N | D |
|---|---|---|---|---|---|---|---|---|---|---|---|

## ADDITIONAL NOTES

## HEAD

| | |
|---|---|
| SPECIES | |
| SEX / AGE | |
| BEHAVIOR | |
| VOICE | |
| BODY | |
| LEGS / FEET | |
| HABITAT | |

## LOCATION

LOCATION NAME

GPS COORDINATES

## MONTH SPOTTED

| J | F | M | A | M | J | J | A | S | O | N | D |
|---|---|---|---|---|---|---|---|---|---|---|---|

## ADDITIONAL NOTES

## PHOTO / SKETCH

## HEAD

| | |
|---|---|
| SPECIES | |
| SEX / AGE | |
| BEHAVIOR | |
| VOICE | |
| BODY | |
| LEGS / FEET | |
| HABITAT | |

## LOCATION

LOCATION NAME

GPS COORDINATES

## MONTH SPOTTED

| J | F | M | A | M | J | J | A | S | O | N | D |
|---|---|---|---|---|---|---|---|---|---|---|---|

## ADDITIONAL NOTES

## PHOTO / SKETCH

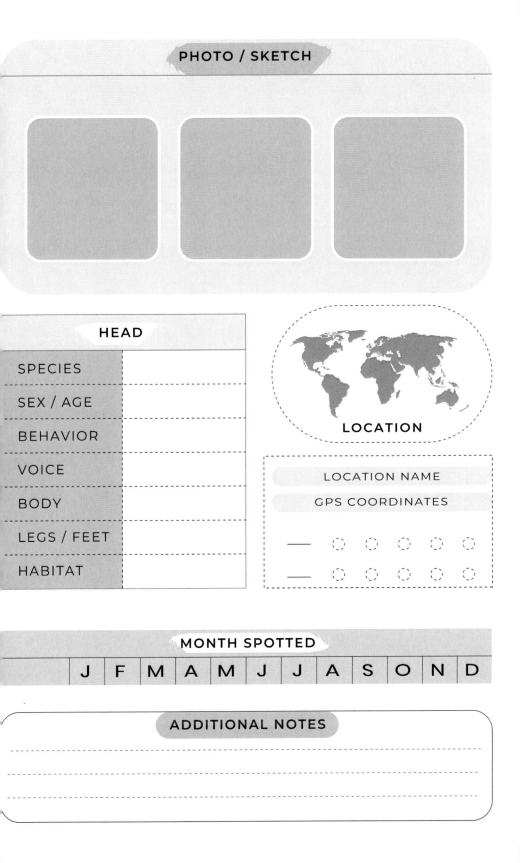

### HEAD

| | |
|---|---|
| SPECIES | |
| SEX / AGE | |
| BEHAVIOR | |
| VOICE | |
| BODY | |
| LEGS / FEET | |
| HABITAT | |

### LOCATION

LOCATION NAME

GPS COORDINATES

— ○ ○ ○ ○ ○

— ○ ○ ○ ○ ○

### MONTH SPOTTED

| J | F | M | A | M | J | J | A | S | O | N | D |
|---|---|---|---|---|---|---|---|---|---|---|---|

### ADDITIONAL NOTES

## PHOTO / SKETCH

| HEAD | |
|---|---|
| SPECIES | |
| SEX / AGE | |
| BEHAVIOR | |
| VOICE | |
| BODY | |
| LEGS / FEET | |
| HABITAT | |

## LOCATION

LOCATION NAME

GPS COORDINATES

— ◌ ◌ ◌ ◌ ◌

— ◌ ◌ ◌ ◌ ◌

## MONTH SPOTTED

| J | F | M | A | M | J | J | A | S | O | N | D |
|---|---|---|---|---|---|---|---|---|---|---|---|

## ADDITIONAL NOTES

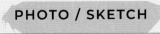

## PHOTO / SKETCH

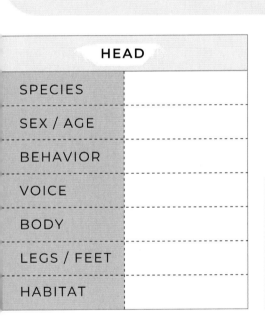

### HEAD

| | |
|---|---|
| SPECIES | |
| SEX / AGE | |
| BEHAVIOR | |
| VOICE | |
| BODY | |
| LEGS / FEET | |
| HABITAT | |

### LOCATION

LOCATION NAME

GPS COORDINATES

— ◌ ◌ ◌ ◌ ◌

— ◌ ◌ ◌ ◌ ◌

## MONTH SPOTTED

| J | F | M | A | M | J | J | A | S | O | N | D |
|---|---|---|---|---|---|---|---|---|---|---|---|

## ADDITIONAL NOTES

## PHOTO / SKETCH

| HEAD | |
|---|---|
| SPECIES | |
| SEX / AGE | |
| BEHAVIOR | |
| VOICE | |
| BODY | |
| LEGS / FEET | |
| HABITAT | |

## LOCATION

LOCATION NAME

GPS COORDINATES

— ○ ○ ○ ○ ○

— ○ ○ ○ ○ ○

## MONTH SPOTTED

| J | F | M | A | M | J | J | A | S | O | N | D |
|---|---|---|---|---|---|---|---|---|---|---|---|

## ADDITIONAL NOTES

## PHOTO / SKETCH

## HEAD

| | |
|---|---|
| SPECIES | |
| SEX / AGE | |
| BEHAVIOR | |
| VOICE | |
| BODY | |
| LEGS / FEET | |
| HABITAT | |

## LOCATION

LOCATION NAME

GPS COORDINATES

___  ○ ○ ○ ○ ○

___  ○ ○ ○ ○ ○

## MONTH SPOTTED

| J | F | M | A | M | J | J | A | S | O | N | D |
|---|---|---|---|---|---|---|---|---|---|---|---|

## ADDITIONAL NOTES

## PHOTO / SKETCH

## HEAD

| | |
|---|---|
| SPECIES | |
| SEX / AGE | |
| BEHAVIOR | |
| VOICE | |
| BODY | |
| LEGS / FEET | |
| HABITAT | |

## LOCATION

LOCATION NAME

GPS COORDINATES

— ○ ○ ○ ○ ○

— ○ ○ ○ ○ ○

## MONTH SPOTTED

| J | F | M | A | M | J | J | A | S | O | N | D |
|---|---|---|---|---|---|---|---|---|---|---|---|

## ADDITIONAL NOTES

## PHOTO / SKETCH

## HEAD

| SPECIES | |
| --- | --- |
| SEX / AGE | |
| BEHAVIOR | |
| VOICE | |
| BODY | |
| LEGS / FEET | |
| HABITAT | |

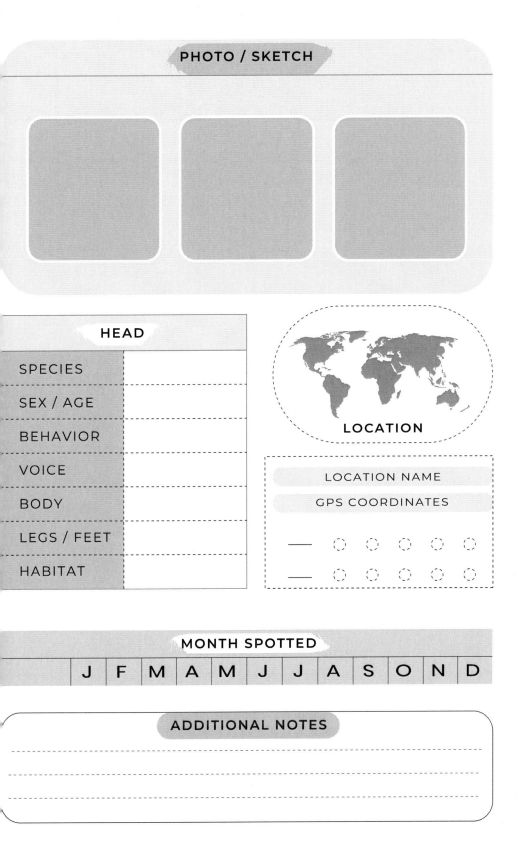

### LOCATION

LOCATION NAME

GPS COORDINATES

## MONTH SPOTTED

| J | F | M | A | M | J | J | A | S | O | N | D |
| --- | --- | --- | --- | --- | --- | --- | --- | --- | --- | --- | --- |

## ADDITIONAL NOTES

# PHOTO / SKETCH

## HEAD

| | |
|---|---|
| SPECIES | |
| SEX / AGE | |
| BEHAVIOR | |
| VOICE | |
| BODY | |
| LEGS / FEET | |
| HABITAT | |

## LOCATION

LOCATION NAME

GPS COORDINATES

## MONTH SPOTTED

| J | F | M | A | M | J | J | A | S | O | N | D |
|---|---|---|---|---|---|---|---|---|---|---|---|

## ADDITIONAL NOTES

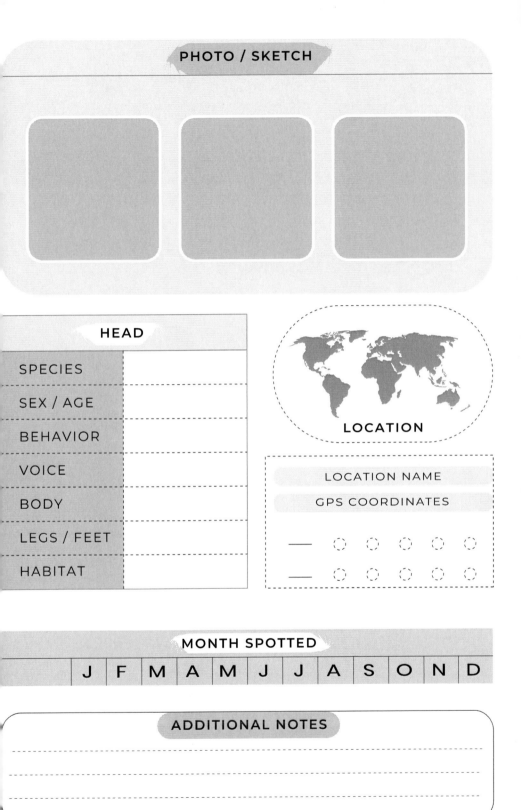

## PHOTO / SKETCH

## HEAD

| | |
|---|---|
| SPECIES | |
| SEX / AGE | |
| BEHAVIOR | |
| VOICE | |
| BODY | |
| LEGS / FEET | |
| HABITAT | |

## LOCATION

LOCATION NAME

GPS COORDINATES

## MONTH SPOTTED

| J | F | M | A | M | J | J | A | S | O | N | D |
|---|---|---|---|---|---|---|---|---|---|---|---|

## ADDITIONAL NOTES

## PHOTO / SKETCH

| HEAD | |
|---|---|
| SPECIES | |
| SEX / AGE | |
| BEHAVIOR | |
| VOICE | |
| BODY | |
| LEGS / FEET | |
| HABITAT | |

### LOCATION

LOCATION NAME

GPS COORDINATES

— ○ ○ ○ ○ ○

— ○ ○ ○ ○ ○

## MONTH SPOTTED

| J | F | M | A | M | J | J | A | S | O | N | D |

## ADDITIONAL NOTES

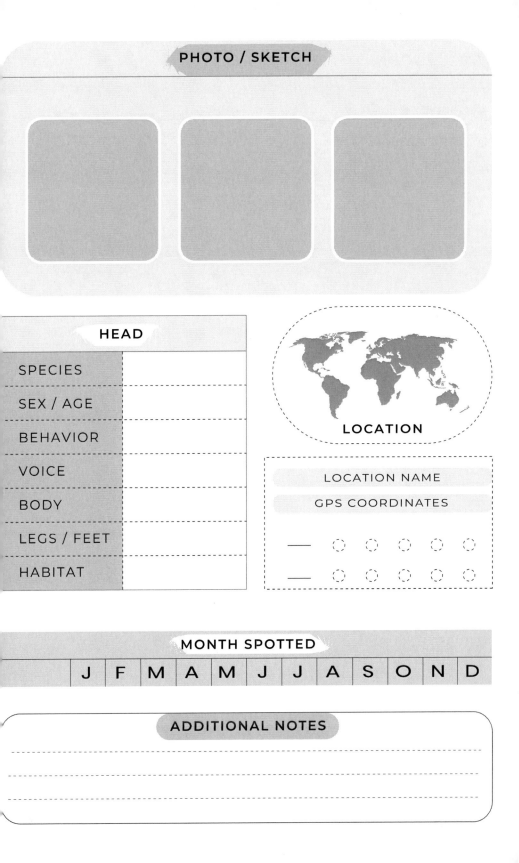

## PHOTO / SKETCH

## HEAD

| | |
|---|---|
| SPECIES | |
| SEX / AGE | |
| BEHAVIOR | |
| VOICE | |
| BODY | |
| LEGS / FEET | |
| HABITAT | |

## LOCATION

LOCATION NAME

GPS COORDINATES

## MONTH SPOTTED

| J | F | M | A | M | J | J | A | S | O | N | D |
|---|---|---|---|---|---|---|---|---|---|---|---|

## ADDITIONAL NOTES

## PHOTO / SKETCH

## HEAD

| | |
|---|---|
| SPECIES | |
| SEX / AGE | |
| BEHAVIOR | |
| VOICE | |
| BODY | |
| LEGS / FEET | |
| HABITAT | |

## LOCATION

LOCATION NAME

GPS COORDINATES

— ○ ○ ○ ○ ○

— ○ ○ ○ ○ ○

## MONTH SPOTTED

| J | F | M | A | M | J | J | A | S | O | N | D |
|---|---|---|---|---|---|---|---|---|---|---|---|

## ADDITIONAL NOTES

## PHOTO / SKETCH

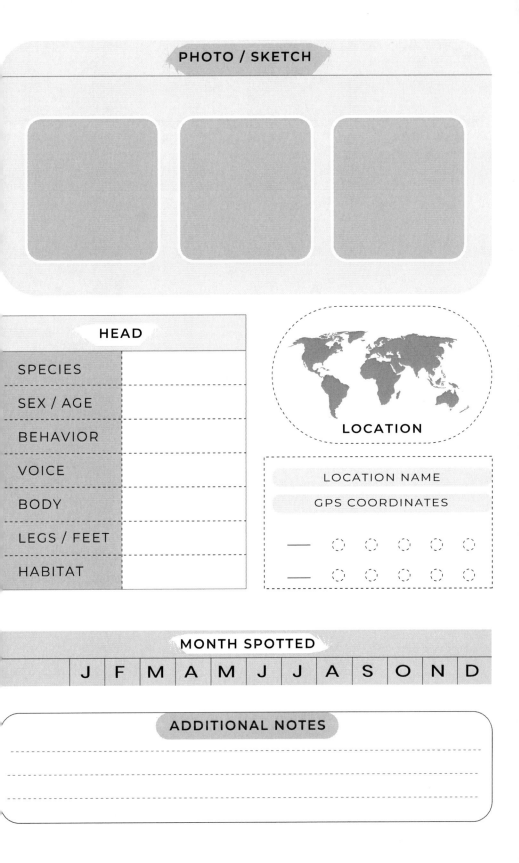

| HEAD | |
|---|---|
| SPECIES | |
| SEX / AGE | |
| BEHAVIOR | |
| VOICE | |
| BODY | |
| LEGS / FEET | |
| HABITAT | |

## LOCATION

LOCATION NAME

GPS COORDINATES

## MONTH SPOTTED

| J | F | M | A | M | J | J | A | S | O | N | D |

## ADDITIONAL NOTES

## PHOTO / SKETCH

## HEAD

| | |
|---|---|
| SPECIES | |
| SEX / AGE | |
| BEHAVIOR | |
| VOICE | |
| BODY | |
| LEGS / FEET | |
| HABITAT | |

## LOCATION

LOCATION NAME

GPS COORDINATES

___ ◌ ◌ ◌ ◌ ◌

___ ◌ ◌ ◌ ◌ ◌

## MONTH SPOTTED

| J | F | M | A | M | J | J | A | S | O | N | D |

## ADDITIONAL NOTES

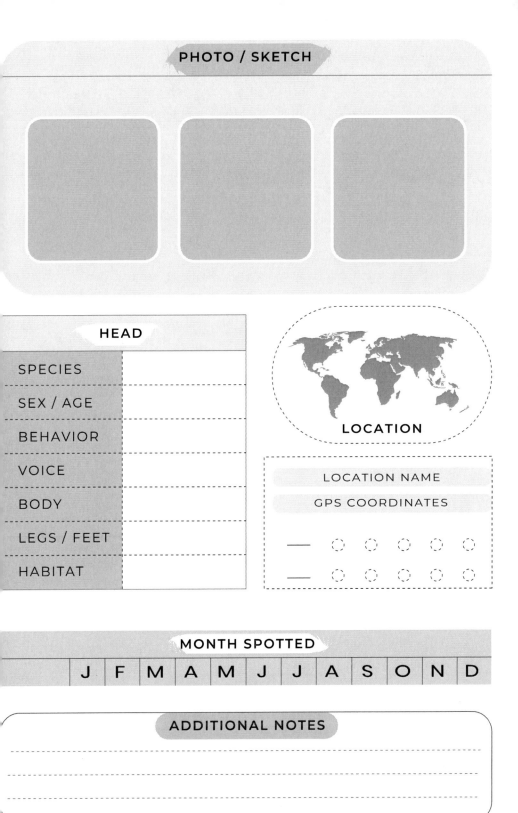

## PHOTO / SKETCH

### HEAD

| | |
|---|---|
| SPECIES | |
| SEX / AGE | |
| BEHAVIOR | |
| VOICE | |
| BODY | |
| LEGS / FEET | |
| HABITAT | |

### LOCATION

LOCATION NAME

GPS COORDINATES

___ ⊙ ⊙ ⊙ ⊙ ⊙
___ ⊙ ⊙ ⊙ ⊙ ⊙

### MONTH SPOTTED

| J | F | M | A | M | J | J | A | S | O | N | D |
|---|---|---|---|---|---|---|---|---|---|---|---|

### ADDITIONAL NOTES

## PHOTO / SKETCH

| HEAD | |
|---|---|
| SPECIES | |
| SEX / AGE | |
| BEHAVIOR | |
| VOICE | |
| BODY | |
| LEGS / FEET | |
| HABITAT | |

## LOCATION

LOCATION NAME

GPS COORDINATES

___  ◌ ◌ ◌ ◌ ◌
___  ◌ ◌ ◌ ◌ ◌

## MONTH SPOTTED

| J | F | M | A | M | J | J | A | S | O | N | D |

## ADDITIONAL NOTES

## PHOTO / SKETCH

### HEAD

| | |
|---|---|
| SPECIES | |
| SEX / AGE | |
| BEHAVIOR | |
| VOICE | |
| BODY | |
| LEGS / FEET | |
| HABITAT | |

### LOCATION

LOCATION NAME

GPS COORDINATES

—  ◌ ◌ ◌ ◌ ◌

—  ◌ ◌ ◌ ◌ ◌

## MONTH SPOTTED

| J | F | M | A | M | J | J | A | S | O | N | D |
|---|---|---|---|---|---|---|---|---|---|---|---|

## ADDITIONAL NOTES

## PHOTO / SKETCH

## HEAD

| | |
|---|---|
| SPECIES | |
| SEX / AGE | |
| BEHAVIOR | |
| VOICE | |
| BODY | |
| LEGS / FEET | |
| HABITAT | |

## LOCATION

LOCATION NAME

GPS COORDINATES

— ◌ ◌ ◌ ◌ ◌

— ◌ ◌ ◌ ◌ ◌

## MONTH SPOTTED

| J | F | M | A | M | J | J | A | S | O | N | D |
|---|---|---|---|---|---|---|---|---|---|---|---|

## ADDITIONAL NOTES

## HEAD

| SPECIES | |
|---|---|
| SEX / AGE | |
| BEHAVIOR | |
| VOICE | |
| BODY | |
| LEGS / FEET | |
| HABITAT | |

## LOCATION

LOCATION NAME

GPS COORDINATES

—  ⊙  ⊙  ⊙  ⊙  ⊙

—  ⊙  ⊙  ⊙  ⊙  ⊙

## MONTH SPOTTED

| J | F | M | A | M | J | J | A | S | O | N | D |
|---|---|---|---|---|---|---|---|---|---|---|---|

## ADDITIONAL NOTES

## PHOTO / SKETCH

| HEAD | |
|---|---|
| SPECIES | |
| SEX / AGE | |
| BEHAVIOR | |
| VOICE | |
| BODY | |
| LEGS / FEET | |
| HABITAT | |

## LOCATION

LOCATION NAME

GPS COORDINATES

___ ◯ ◯ ◯ ◯ ◯

___ ◯ ◯ ◯ ◯ ◯

## MONTH SPOTTED

| J | F | M | A | M | J | J | A | S | O | N | D |

## ADDITIONAL NOTES

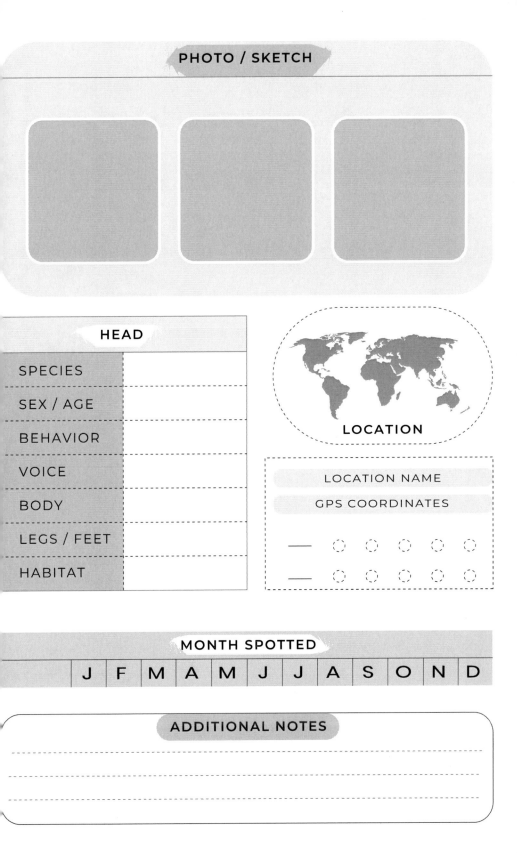

## PHOTO / SKETCH

## HEAD

| | |
|---|---|
| SPECIES | |
| SEX / AGE | |
| BEHAVIOR | |
| VOICE | |
| BODY | |
| LEGS / FEET | |
| HABITAT | |

## LOCATION

LOCATION NAME

GPS COORDINATES

## MONTH SPOTTED

J F M A M J J A S O N D

## ADDITIONAL NOTES

## PHOTO / SKETCH

| HEAD | |
|------|---|
| SPECIES | |
| SEX / AGE | |
| BEHAVIOR | |
| VOICE | |
| BODY | |
| LEGS / FEET | |
| HABITAT | |

### LOCATION

LOCATION NAME

GPS COORDINATES

— ○ ○ ○ ○ ○

— ○ ○ ○ ○ ○

## MONTH SPOTTED

| J | F | M | A | M | J | J | A | S | O | N | D |
|---|---|---|---|---|---|---|---|---|---|---|---|

## ADDITIONAL NOTES

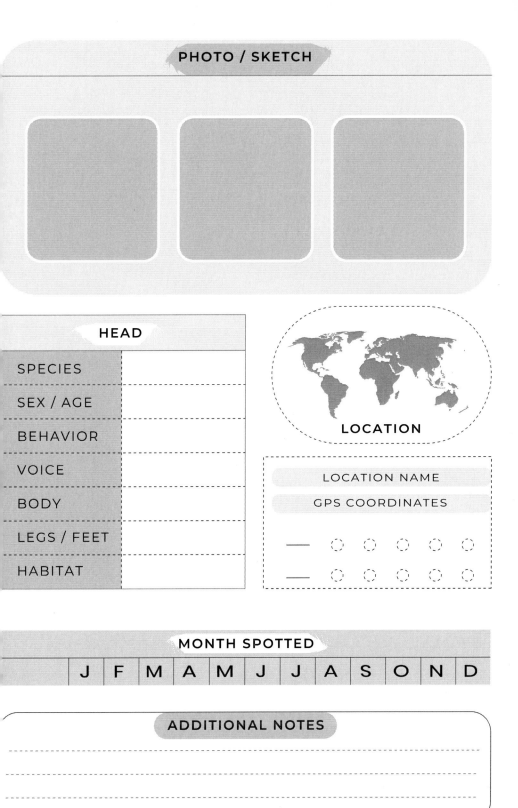

**PHOTO / SKETCH**

**HEAD**

| | |
|---|---|
| SPECIES | |
| SEX / AGE | |
| BEHAVIOR | |
| VOICE | |
| BODY | |
| LEGS / FEET | |
| HABITAT | |

**LOCATION**

LOCATION NAME

GPS COORDINATES

**MONTH SPOTTED**

| J | F | M | A | M | J | J | A | S | O | N | D |
|---|---|---|---|---|---|---|---|---|---|---|---|

**ADDITIONAL NOTES**

## PHOTO / SKETCH

| HEAD | |
|---|---|
| SPECIES | |
| SEX / AGE | |
| BEHAVIOR | |
| VOICE | |
| BODY | |
| LEGS / FEET | |
| HABITAT | |

### LOCATION

LOCATION NAME

GPS COORDINATES

___ ○ ○ ○ ○ ○

___ ○ ○ ○ ○ ○

## MONTH SPOTTED

| J | F | M | A | M | J | J | A | S | O | N | D |
|---|---|---|---|---|---|---|---|---|---|---|---|

## ADDITIONAL NOTES

## PHOTO / SKETCH

## HEAD

| | |
|---|---|
| SPECIES | |
| SEX / AGE | |
| BEHAVIOR | |
| VOICE | |
| BODY | |
| LEGS / FEET | |
| HABITAT | |

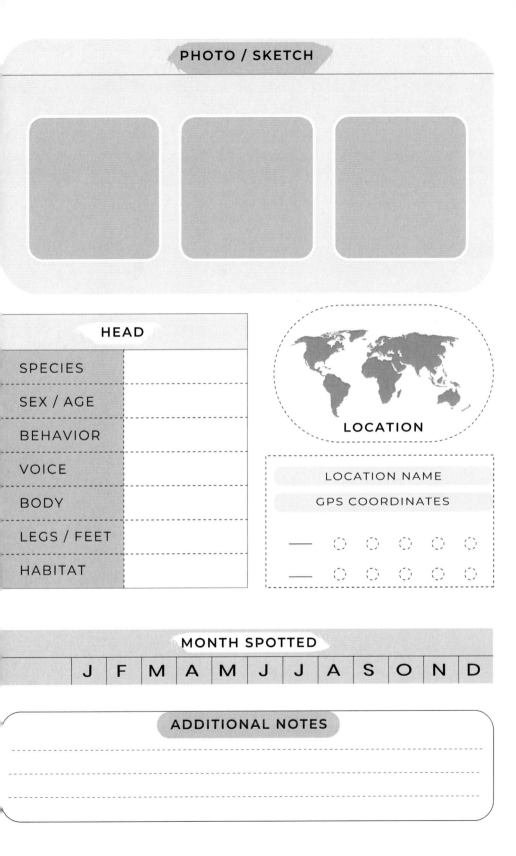

## LOCATION

LOCATION NAME

GPS COORDINATES

___ ○ ○ ○ ○ ○

___ ○ ○ ○ ○ ○

## MONTH SPOTTED

| J | F | M | A | M | J | J | A | S | O | N | D |
|---|---|---|---|---|---|---|---|---|---|---|---|

## ADDITIONAL NOTES

## PHOTO / SKETCH

### HEAD

| | |
|---|---|
| SPECIES | |
| SEX / AGE | |
| BEHAVIOR | |
| VOICE | |
| BODY | |
| LEGS / FEET | |
| HABITAT | |

### LOCATION

LOCATION NAME

GPS COORDINATES

## MONTH SPOTTED

| J | F | M | A | M | J | J | A | S | O | N | D |
|---|---|---|---|---|---|---|---|---|---|---|---|

## ADDITIONAL NOTES

## HEAD

| SPECIES | |
|---|---|
| SEX / AGE | |
| BEHAVIOR | |
| VOICE | |
| BODY | |
| LEGS / FEET | |
| HABITAT | |

## LOCATION

LOCATION NAME

GPS COORDINATES

— ○ ○ ○ ○ ○
— ○ ○ ○ ○ ○

## MONTH SPOTTED

| J | F | M | A | M | J | J | A | S | O | N | D |

## ADDITIONAL NOTES

## PHOTO / SKETCH

### HEAD

| | |
|---|---|
| SPECIES | |
| SEX / AGE | |
| BEHAVIOR | |
| VOICE | |
| BODY | |
| LEGS / FEET | |
| HABITAT | |

### LOCATION

LOCATION NAME

GPS COORDINATES

—  ○  ○  ○  ○  ○

—  ○  ○  ○  ○  ○

## MONTH SPOTTED

| J | F | M | A | M | J | J | A | S | O | N | D |
|---|---|---|---|---|---|---|---|---|---|---|---|

## ADDITIONAL NOTES

## PHOTO / SKETCH

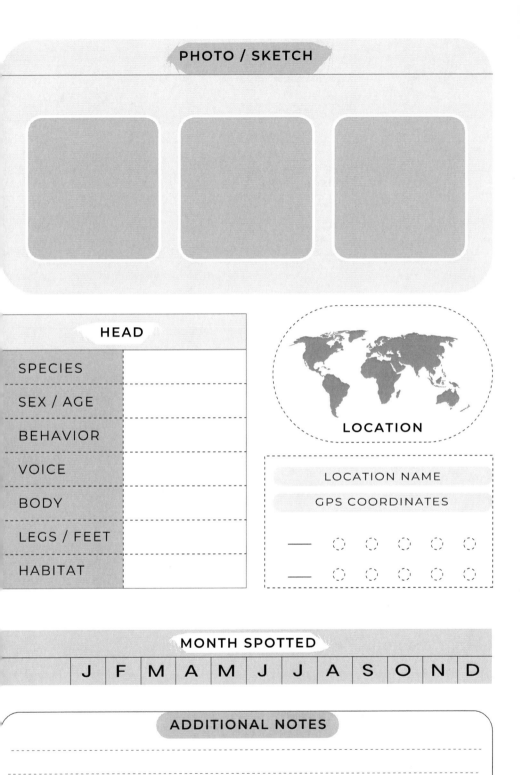

## HEAD

| | |
|---|---|
| SPECIES | |
| SEX / AGE | |
| BEHAVIOR | |
| VOICE | |
| BODY | |
| LEGS / FEET | |
| HABITAT | |

## LOCATION

LOCATION NAME

GPS COORDINATES

## MONTH SPOTTED

| J | F | M | A | M | J | J | A | S | O | N | D |
|---|---|---|---|---|---|---|---|---|---|---|---|

## ADDITIONAL NOTES

# PHOTO / SKETCH

## HEAD

| | |
|---|---|
| SPECIES | |
| SEX / AGE | |
| BEHAVIOR | |
| VOICE | |
| BODY | |
| LEGS / FEET | |
| HABITAT | |

## LOCATION

LOCATION NAME

GPS COORDINATES

— ○ ○ ○ ○ ○

— ○ ○ ○ ○ ○

## MONTH SPOTTED

| J | F | M | A | M | J | J | A | S | O | N | D |
|---|---|---|---|---|---|---|---|---|---|---|---|

## ADDITIONAL NOTES

## PHOTO / SKETCH

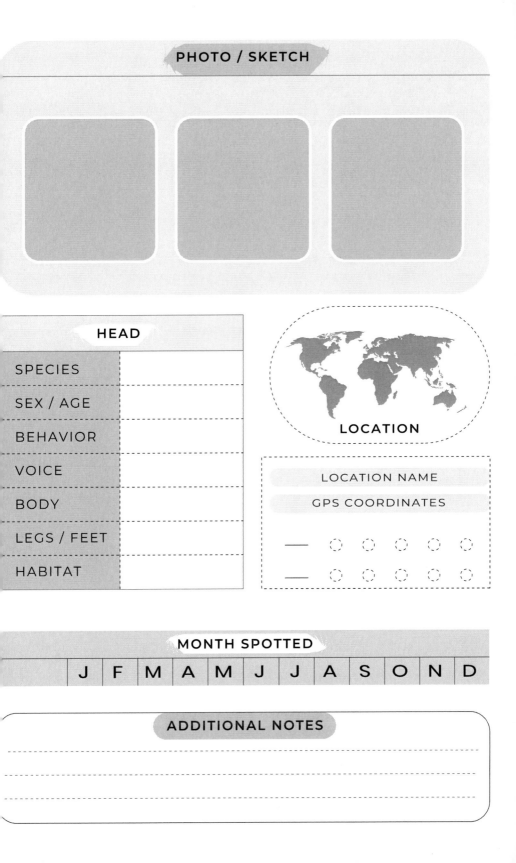

## HEAD

| | |
|---|---|
| SPECIES | |
| SEX / AGE | |
| BEHAVIOR | |
| VOICE | |
| BODY | |
| LEGS / FEET | |
| HABITAT | |

## LOCATION

LOCATION NAME

GPS COORDINATES

## MONTH SPOTTED

| J | F | M | A | M | J | J | A | S | O | N | D |
|---|---|---|---|---|---|---|---|---|---|---|---|

## ADDITIONAL NOTES

## PHOTO / SKETCH

| HEAD | |
|---|---|
| SPECIES | |
| SEX / AGE | |
| BEHAVIOR | |
| VOICE | |
| BODY | |
| LEGS / FEET | |
| HABITAT | |

## LOCATION

LOCATION NAME

GPS COORDINATES

___ ○ ○ ○ ○ ○

___ ○ ○ ○ ○ ○

## MONTH SPOTTED

| J | F | M | A | M | J | J | A | S | O | N | D |

## ADDITIONAL NOTES

## PHOTO / SKETCH

## HEAD

| | |
|---|---|
| SPECIES | |
| SEX / AGE | |
| BEHAVIOR | |
| VOICE | |
| BODY | |
| LEGS / FEET | |
| HABITAT | |

## LOCATION

LOCATION NAME

GPS COORDINATES

— ○ ○ ○ ○ ○

— ○ ○ ○ ○ ○

## MONTH SPOTTED

| J | F | M | A | M | J | J | A | S | O | N | D |
|---|---|---|---|---|---|---|---|---|---|---|---|

## ADDITIONAL NOTES

## PHOTO / SKETCH

| HEAD | |
|---|---|
| SPECIES | |
| SEX / AGE | |
| BEHAVIOR | |
| VOICE | |
| BODY | |
| LEGS / FEET | |
| HABITAT | |

### LOCATION

LOCATION NAME

GPS COORDINATES

## MONTH SPOTTED

| J | F | M | A | M | J | J | A | S | O | N | D |
|---|---|---|---|---|---|---|---|---|---|---|---|

## ADDITIONAL NOTES

## PHOTO / SKETCH

## HEAD

| SPECIES | |
| --- | --- |
| SEX / AGE | |
| BEHAVIOR | |
| VOICE | |
| BODY | |
| LEGS / FEET | |
| HABITAT | |

## LOCATION

| LOCATION NAME | |
| --- | --- |
| GPS COORDINATES | |

## MONTH SPOTTED

| J | F | M | A | M | J | J | A | S | O | N | D |
| --- | --- | --- | --- | --- | --- | --- | --- | --- | --- | --- | --- |

## ADDITIONAL NOTES

| HEAD | |
|---|---|
| SPECIES | |
| SEX / AGE | |
| BEHAVIOR | |
| VOICE | |
| BODY | |
| LEGS / FEET | |
| HABITAT | |

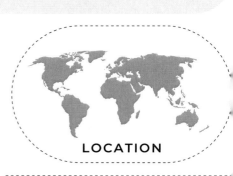

**LOCATION**

LOCATION NAME

GPS COORDINATES

___ ◌ ◌ ◌ ◌ ◌

___ ◌ ◌ ◌ ◌ ◌

**MONTH SPOTTED**

| J | F | M | A | M | J | J | A | S | O | N | D |
|---|---|---|---|---|---|---|---|---|---|---|---|

**ADDITIONAL NOTES**

## PHOTO / SKETCH

### HEAD

| | |
|---|---|
| SPECIES | |
| SEX / AGE | |
| BEHAVIOR | |
| VOICE | |
| BODY | |
| LEGS / FEET | |
| HABITAT | |

### LOCATION

LOCATION NAME

GPS COORDINATES

___ ○ ○ ○ ○ ○

___ ○ ○ ○ ○ ○

### MONTH SPOTTED

| J | F | M | A | M | J | J | A | S | O | N | D |
|---|---|---|---|---|---|---|---|---|---|---|---|

### ADDITIONAL NOTES

## HEAD

| | |
|---|---|
| SPECIES | |
| SEX / AGE | |
| BEHAVIOR | |
| VOICE | |
| BODY | |
| LEGS / FEET | |
| HABITAT | |

## LOCATION

LOCATION NAME

GPS COORDINATES

_____ ○ ○ ○ ○ ○

_____ ○ ○ ○ ○ ○

## MONTH SPOTTED

| J | F | M | A | M | J | J | A | S | O | N | D |
|---|---|---|---|---|---|---|---|---|---|---|---|

## ADDITIONAL NOTES

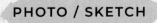

### HEAD

| | |
|---|---|
| SPECIES | |
| SEX / AGE | |
| BEHAVIOR | |
| VOICE | |
| BODY | |
| LEGS / FEET | |
| HABITAT | |

### LOCATION

LOCATION NAME

GPS COORDINATES

## MONTH SPOTTED

| J | F | M | A | M | J | J | A | S | O | N | D |
|---|---|---|---|---|---|---|---|---|---|---|---|

## ADDITIONAL NOTES

| HEAD | |
|---|---|
| SPECIES | |
| SEX / AGE | |
| BEHAVIOR | |
| VOICE | |
| BODY | |
| LEGS / FEET | |
| HABITAT | |

LOCATION

LOCATION NAME

GPS COORDINATES

___ ○ ○ ○ ○ ○

___ ○ ○ ○ ○ ○

## MONTH SPOTTED

| J | F | M | A | M | J | J | A | S | O | N | D |

## ADDITIONAL NOTES

## PHOTO / SKETCH

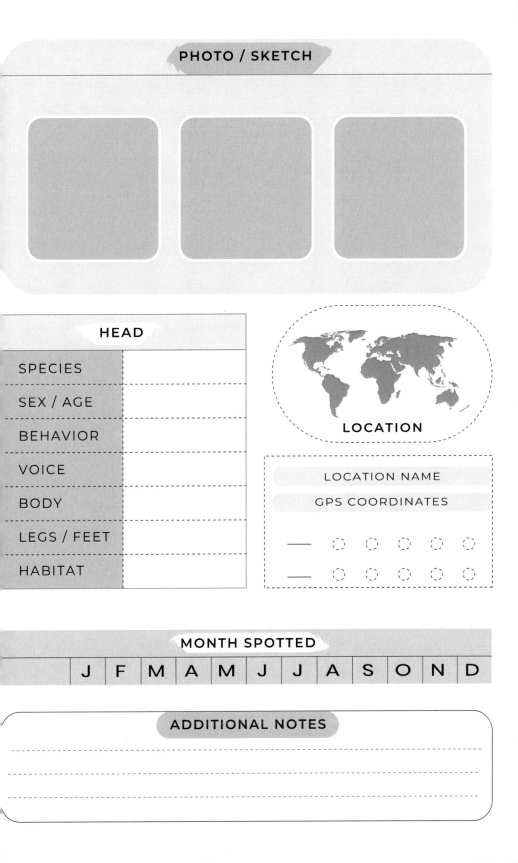

## HEAD

| | |
|---|---|
| SPECIES | |
| SEX / AGE | |
| BEHAVIOR | |
| VOICE | |
| BODY | |
| LEGS / FEET | |
| HABITAT | |

## LOCATION

LOCATION NAME

GPS COORDINATES

## MONTH SPOTTED

| J | F | M | A | M | J | J | A | S | O | N | D |
|---|---|---|---|---|---|---|---|---|---|---|---|

## ADDITIONAL NOTES

| HEAD | |
|---|---|
| SPECIES | |
| SEX / AGE | |
| BEHAVIOR | |
| VOICE | |
| BODY | |
| LEGS / FEET | |
| HABITAT | |

### LOCATION

LOCATION NAME

GPS COORDINATES

— ○ ○ ○ ○ ○

— ○ ○ ○ ○ ○

## MONTH SPOTTED

| J | F | M | A | M | J | J | A | S | O | N | D |
|---|---|---|---|---|---|---|---|---|---|---|---|

## ADDITIONAL NOTES

## PHOTO / SKETCH

## HEAD

| | |
|---|---|
| SPECIES | |
| SEX / AGE | |
| BEHAVIOR | |
| VOICE | |
| BODY | |
| LEGS / FEET | |
| HABITAT | |

## LOCATION

LOCATION NAME

GPS COORDINATES

— ○ ○ ○ ○ ○

— ○ ○ ○ ○ ○

## MONTH SPOTTED

| J | F | M | A | M | J | J | A | S | O | N | D |
|---|---|---|---|---|---|---|---|---|---|---|---|

## ADDITIONAL NOTES

## PHOTO / SKETCH

| HEAD | |
|---|---|
| SPECIES | |
| SEX / AGE | |
| BEHAVIOR | |
| VOICE | |
| BODY | |
| LEGS / FEET | |
| HABITAT | |

### LOCATION

LOCATION NAME

GPS COORDINATES

— ◯ ◯ ◯ ◯ ◯

— ◯ ◯ ◯ ◯ ◯

## MONTH SPOTTED

| J | F | M | A | M | J | J | A | S | O | N | D |
|---|---|---|---|---|---|---|---|---|---|---|---|

## ADDITIONAL NOTES

## PHOTO / SKETCH

## HEAD

| | |
|---|---|
| SPECIES | |
| SEX / AGE | |
| BEHAVIOR | |
| VOICE | |
| BODY | |
| LEGS / FEET | |
| HABITAT | |

## LOCATION

LOCATION NAME

GPS COORDINATES

— ○ ○ ○ ○ ○

— ○ ○ ○ ○ ○

## MONTH SPOTTED

| J | F | M | A | M | J | J | A | S | O | N | D |
|---|---|---|---|---|---|---|---|---|---|---|---|

## ADDITIONAL NOTES

## PHOTO / SKETCH

## HEAD

| | |
|---|---|
| SPECIES | |
| SEX / AGE | |
| BEHAVIOR | |
| VOICE | |
| BODY | |
| LEGS / FEET | |
| HABITAT | |

## LOCATION

LOCATION NAME

GPS COORDINATES

— ○ ○ ○ ○ ○

— ○ ○ ○ ○ ○

## MONTH SPOTTED

| J | F | M | A | M | J | J | A | S | O | N | D |
|---|---|---|---|---|---|---|---|---|---|---|---|

## ADDITIONAL NOTES

## PHOTO / SKETCH

## HEAD

| | |
|---|---|
| SPECIES | |
| SEX / AGE | |
| BEHAVIOR | |
| VOICE | |
| BODY | |
| LEGS / FEET | |
| HABITAT | |

## LOCATION

LOCATION NAME

GPS COORDINATES

— ○ ○ ○ ○ ○

— ○ ○ ○ ○ ○

## MONTH SPOTTED

| J | F | M | A | M | J | J | A | S | O | N | D |
|---|---|---|---|---|---|---|---|---|---|---|---|

## ADDITIONAL NOTES

## PHOTO / SKETCH

| HEAD | |
|---|---|
| SPECIES | |
| SEX / AGE | |
| BEHAVIOR | |
| VOICE | |
| BODY | |
| LEGS / FEET | |
| HABITAT | |

**LOCATION**

LOCATION NAME

GPS COORDINATES

— ◯ ◯ ◯ ◯ ◯

— ◯ ◯ ◯ ◯ ◯

## MONTH SPOTTED

| J | F | M | A | M | J | J | A | S | O | N | D |
|---|---|---|---|---|---|---|---|---|---|---|---|

## ADDITIONAL NOTES

## PHOTO / SKETCH

## HEAD

| | |
|---|---|
| SPECIES | |
| SEX / AGE | |
| BEHAVIOR | |
| VOICE | |
| BODY | |
| LEGS / FEET | |
| HABITAT | |

## LOCATION

LOCATION NAME

GPS COORDINATES

## MONTH SPOTTED

| J | F | M | A | M | J | J | A | S | O | N | D |
|---|---|---|---|---|---|---|---|---|---|---|---|

## ADDITIONAL NOTES

## HEAD

| | |
|---|---|
| SPECIES | |
| SEX / AGE | |
| BEHAVIOR | |
| VOICE | |
| BODY | |
| LEGS / FEET | |
| HABITAT | |

### LOCATION

LOCATION NAME

GPS COORDINATES

— ◯ ◯ ◯ ◯ ◯

— ◯ ◯ ◯ ◯ ◯

## MONTH SPOTTED

| J | F | M | A | M | J | J | A | S | O | N | D |
|---|---|---|---|---|---|---|---|---|---|---|---|

## ADDITIONAL NOTES

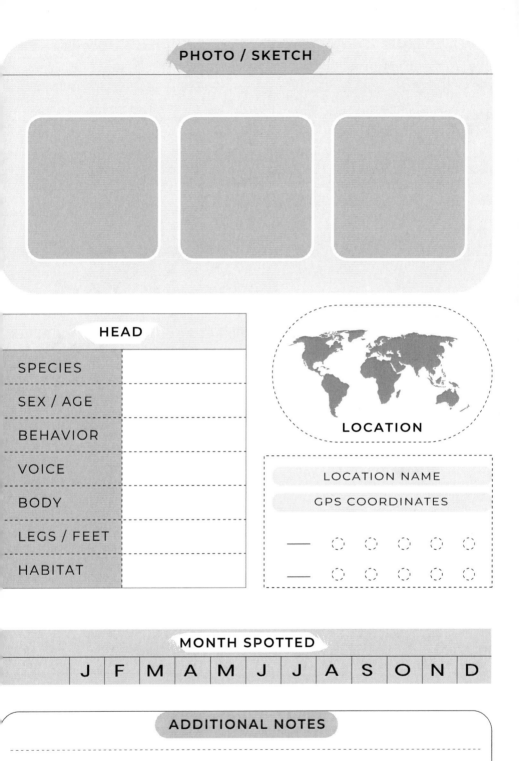

## PHOTO / SKETCH

## HEAD

| SPECIES | |
|---|---|
| SEX / AGE | |
| BEHAVIOR | |
| VOICE | |
| BODY | |
| LEGS / FEET | |
| HABITAT | |

## LOCATION

LOCATION NAME

GPS COORDINATES

— ○ ○ ○ ○ ○

— ○ ○ ○ ○ ○

## MONTH SPOTTED

| J | F | M | A | M | J | J | A | S | O | N | D |
|---|---|---|---|---|---|---|---|---|---|---|---|

## ADDITIONAL NOTES

## PHOTO / SKETCH

| HEAD | |
|---|---|
| SPECIES | |
| SEX / AGE | |
| BEHAVIOR | |
| VOICE | |
| BODY | |
| LEGS / FEET | |
| HABITAT | |

**LOCATION**

LOCATION NAME

GPS COORDINATES

— ⊙ ⊙ ⊙ ⊙ ⊙

— ⊙ ⊙ ⊙ ⊙ ⊙

## MONTH SPOTTED

| J | F | M | A | M | J | J | A | S | O | N | D |

## ADDITIONAL NOTES

# PHOTO / SKETCH

## HEAD

| | |
|---|---|
| SPECIES | |
| SEX / AGE | |
| BEHAVIOR | |
| VOICE | |
| BODY | |
| LEGS / FEET | |
| HABITAT | |

## LOCATION

LOCATION NAME

GPS COORDINATES

## MONTH SPOTTED

| J | F | M | A | M | J | J | A | S | O | N | D |
|---|---|---|---|---|---|---|---|---|---|---|---|

## ADDITIONAL NOTES

### HEAD

| | |
|---|---|
| SPECIES | |
| SEX / AGE | |
| BEHAVIOR | |
| VOICE | |
| BODY | |
| LEGS / FEET | |
| HABITAT | |

### LOCATION

LOCATION NAME

GPS COORDINATES

—  ○ ○ ○ ○ ○

—  ○ ○ ○ ○ ○

### MONTH SPOTTED

| J | F | M | A | M | J | J | A | S | O | N | D |
|---|---|---|---|---|---|---|---|---|---|---|---|

### ADDITIONAL NOTES

## HEAD

| | |
|---|---|
| SPECIES | |
| SEX / AGE | |
| BEHAVIOR | |
| VOICE | |
| BODY | |
| LEGS / FEET | |
| HABITAT | |

**LOCATION**

LOCATION NAME

GPS COORDINATES

— ◯ ◯ ◯ ◯ ◯

— ◯ ◯ ◯ ◯ ◯

## MONTH SPOTTED

| J | F | M | A | M | J | J | A | S | O | N | D |
|---|---|---|---|---|---|---|---|---|---|---|---|

## ADDITIONAL NOTES

| HEAD | |
|---|---|
| SPECIES | |
| SEX / AGE | |
| BEHAVIOR | |
| VOICE | |
| BODY | |
| LEGS / FEET | |
| HABITAT | |

### LOCATION

LOCATION NAME

GPS COORDINATES

___ ○ ○ ○ ○ ○

___ ○ ○ ○ ○ ○

## MONTH SPOTTED

| J | F | M | A | M | J | J | A | S | O | N | D |

## ADDITIONAL NOTES

## HEAD

| | |
|---|---|
| SPECIES | |
| SEX / AGE | |
| BEHAVIOR | |
| VOICE | |
| BODY | |
| LEGS / FEET | |
| HABITAT | |

### LOCATION

LOCATION NAME

GPS COORDINATES

—  ○ ○ ○ ○ ○

—  ○ ○ ○ ○ ○

## MONTH SPOTTED

| J | F | M | A | M | J | J | A | S | O | N | D |
|---|---|---|---|---|---|---|---|---|---|---|---|

## ADDITIONAL NOTES

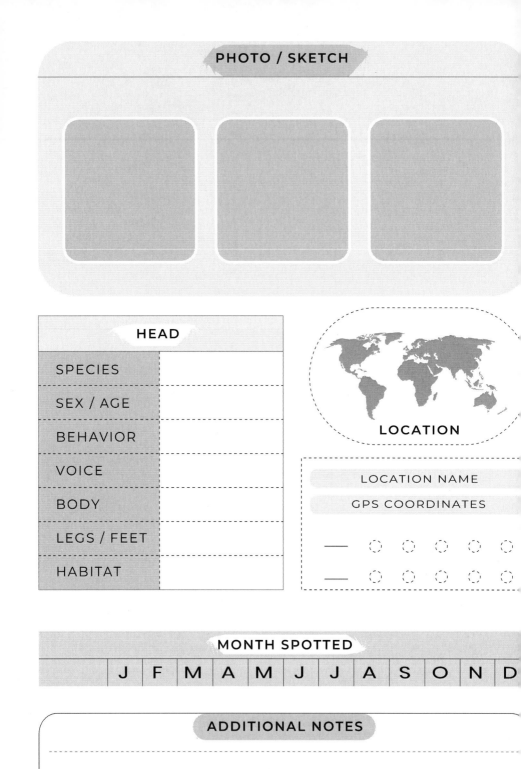

## PHOTO / SKETCH

## HEAD

| | |
|---|---|
| SPECIES | |
| SEX / AGE | |
| BEHAVIOR | |
| VOICE | |
| BODY | |
| LEGS / FEET | |
| HABITAT | |

## LOCATION

LOCATION NAME

GPS COORDINATES

## MONTH SPOTTED

| J | F | M | A | M | J | J | A | S | O | N | D |
|---|---|---|---|---|---|---|---|---|---|---|---|

## ADDITIONAL NOTES

## PHOTO / SKETCH

## HEAD

| | |
|---|---|
| SPECIES | |
| SEX / AGE | |
| BEHAVIOR | |
| VOICE | |
| BODY | |
| LEGS / FEET | |
| HABITAT | |

## LOCATION

LOCATION NAME

GPS COORDINATES

— ○ ○ ○ ○ ○

— ○ ○ ○ ○ ○

## MONTH SPOTTED

| J | F | M | A | M | J | J | A | S | O | N | D |
|---|---|---|---|---|---|---|---|---|---|---|---|

## ADDITIONAL NOTES

## PHOTO / SKETCH

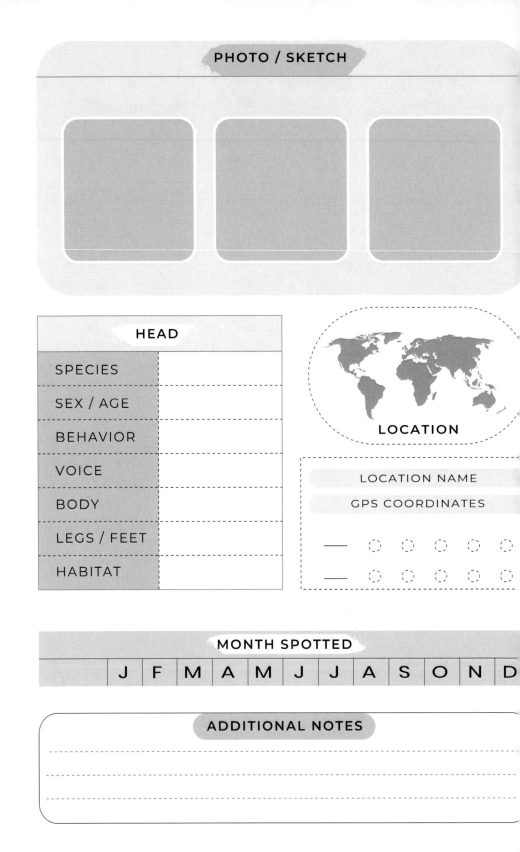

### HEAD

| | |
|---|---|
| SPECIES | |
| SEX / AGE | |
| BEHAVIOR | |
| VOICE | |
| BODY | |
| LEGS / FEET | |
| HABITAT | |

### LOCATION

LOCATION NAME

GPS COORDINATES

## MONTH SPOTTED

| J | F | M | A | M | J | J | A | S | O | N | D |
|---|---|---|---|---|---|---|---|---|---|---|---|

## ADDITIONAL NOTES

## PHOTO / SKETCH

## HEAD

| SPECIES | |
|---|---|
| SEX / AGE | |
| BEHAVIOR | |
| VOICE | |
| BODY | |
| LEGS / FEET | |
| HABITAT | |

## LOCATION

LOCATION NAME

GPS COORDINATES

— ◌ ◌ ◌ ◌ ◌
— ◌ ◌ ◌ ◌ ◌

## MONTH SPOTTED

| J | F | M | A | M | J | J | A | S | O | N | D |
|---|---|---|---|---|---|---|---|---|---|---|---|

## ADDITIONAL NOTES

## PHOTO / SKETCH

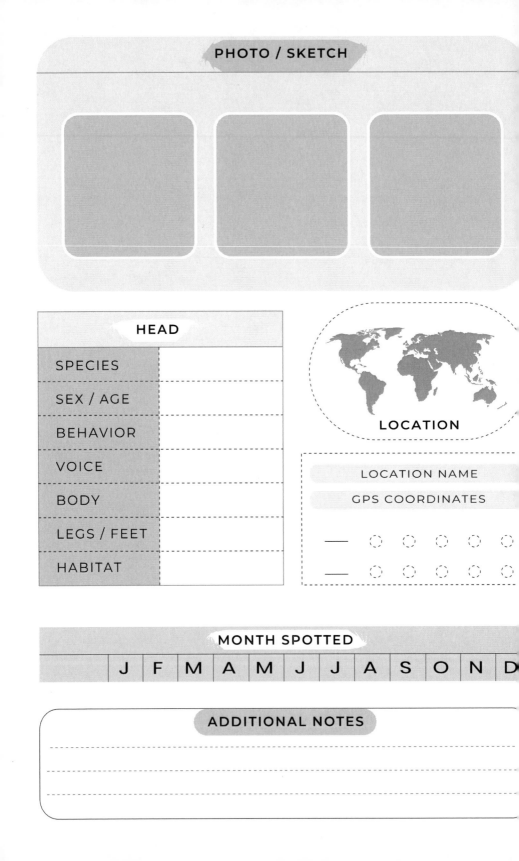

| HEAD | |
|------|------|
| SPECIES | |
| SEX / AGE | |
| BEHAVIOR | |
| VOICE | |
| BODY | |
| LEGS / FEET | |
| HABITAT | |

### LOCATION

LOCATION NAME

GPS COORDINATES

## MONTH SPOTTED

| J | F | M | A | M | J | J | A | S | O | N | D |
|---|---|---|---|---|---|---|---|---|---|---|---|

## ADDITIONAL NOTES

## PHOTO / SKETCH

## HEAD

| | |
|---|---|
| SPECIES | |
| SEX / AGE | |
| BEHAVIOR | |
| VOICE | |
| BODY | |
| LEGS / FEET | |
| HABITAT | |

## LOCATION

LOCATION NAME

GPS COORDINATES

— ◌ ◌ ◌ ◌ ◌

— ◌ ◌ ◌ ◌ ◌

## MONTH SPOTTED

| J | F | M | A | M | J | J | A | S | O | N | D |
|---|---|---|---|---|---|---|---|---|---|---|---|

## ADDITIONAL NOTES

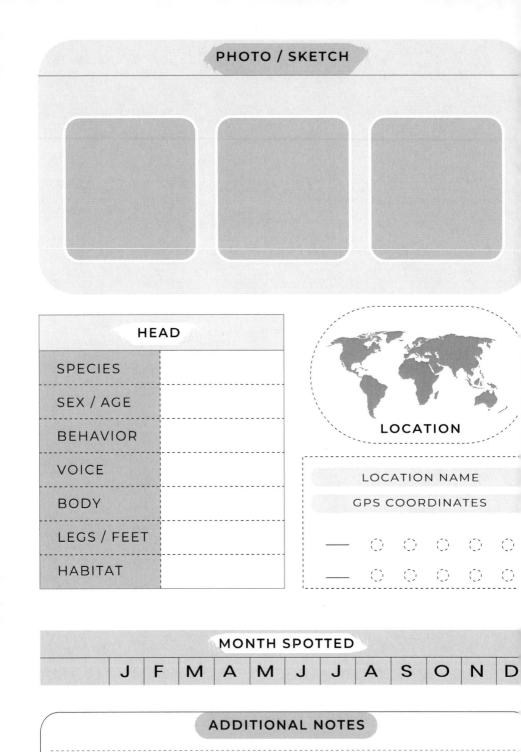

# PHOTO / SKETCH

## HEAD

| | |
|---|---|
| SPECIES | |
| SEX / AGE | |
| BEHAVIOR | |
| VOICE | |
| BODY | |
| LEGS / FEET | |
| HABITAT | |

## LOCATION

LOCATION NAME

GPS COORDINATES

## MONTH SPOTTED

| J | F | M | A | M | J | J | A | S | O | N | D |
|---|---|---|---|---|---|---|---|---|---|---|---|

## ADDITIONAL NOTES

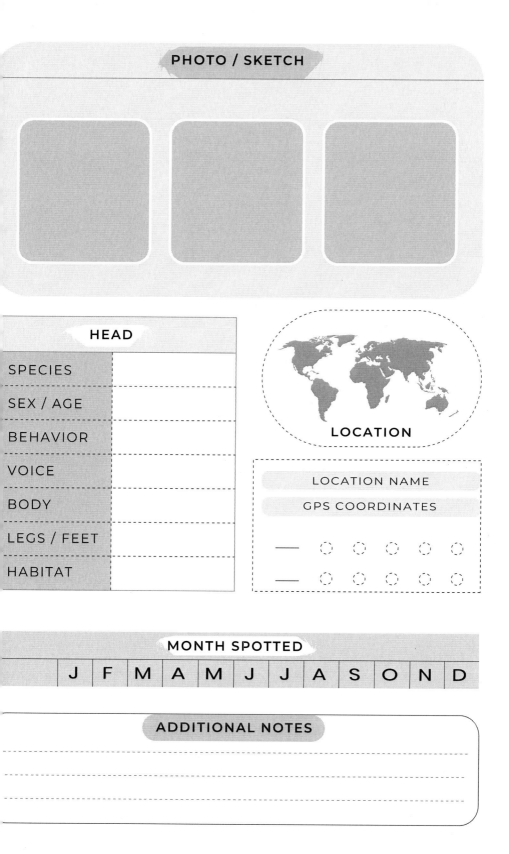

## PHOTO / SKETCH

## HEAD

| | |
|---|---|
| SPECIES | |
| SEX / AGE | |
| BEHAVIOR | |
| VOICE | |
| BODY | |
| LEGS / FEET | |
| HABITAT | |

## LOCATION

LOCATION NAME

GPS COORDINATES

## MONTH SPOTTED

| J | F | M | A | M | J | J | A | S | O | N | D |
|---|---|---|---|---|---|---|---|---|---|---|---|

## ADDITIONAL NOTES

## PHOTO / SKETCH

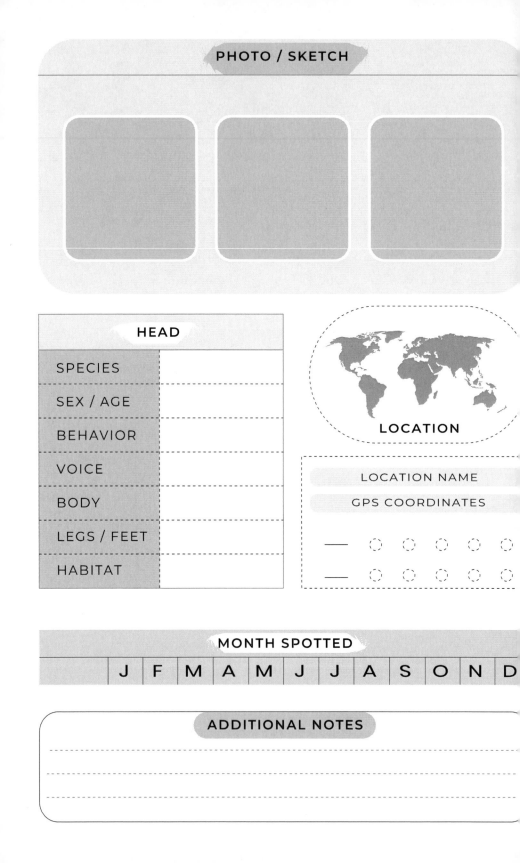

### HEAD

| | |
|---|---|
| SPECIES | |
| SEX / AGE | |
| BEHAVIOR | |
| VOICE | |
| BODY | |
| LEGS / FEET | |
| HABITAT | |

### LOCATION

LOCATION NAME

GPS COORDINATES

## MONTH SPOTTED

| J | F | M | A | M | J | J | A | S | O | N | D |
|---|---|---|---|---|---|---|---|---|---|---|---|

## ADDITIONAL NOTES

## PHOTO / SKETCH

## HEAD

| | |
|---|---|
| SPECIES | |
| SEX / AGE | |
| BEHAVIOR | |
| VOICE | |
| BODY | |
| LEGS / FEET | |
| HABITAT | |

## LOCATION

LOCATION NAME

GPS COORDINATES

— ◌ ◌ ◌ ◌ ◌

— ◌ ◌ ◌ ◌ ◌

## MONTH SPOTTED

| J | F | M | A | M | J | J | A | S | O | N | D |
|---|---|---|---|---|---|---|---|---|---|---|---|

## ADDITIONAL NOTES

# PHOTO / SKETCH

## HEAD

| | |
|---|---|
| SPECIES | |
| SEX / AGE | |
| BEHAVIOR | |
| VOICE | |
| BODY | |
| LEGS / FEET | |
| HABITAT | |

## LOCATION

LOCATION NAME

GPS COORDINATES

## MONTH SPOTTED

| J | F | M | A | M | J | J | A | S | O | N | D |
|---|---|---|---|---|---|---|---|---|---|---|---|

## ADDITIONAL NOTES

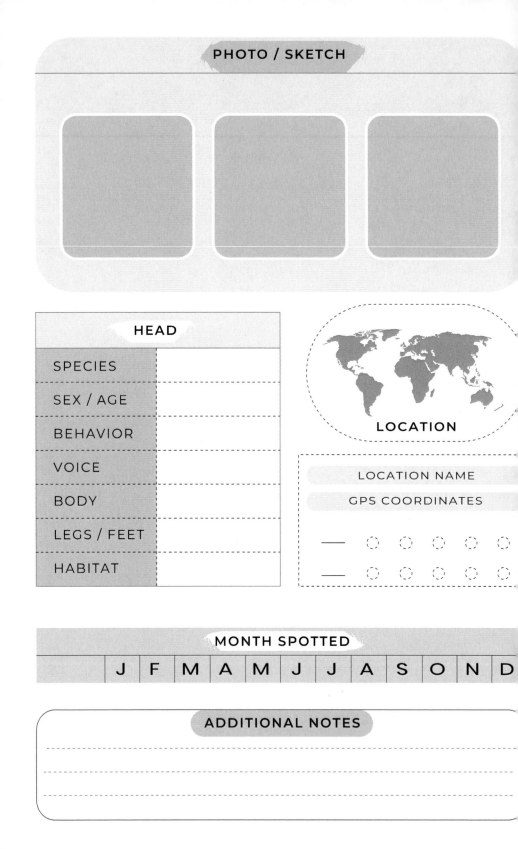

## HEAD

| | |
|---|---|
| SPECIES | |
| SEX / AGE | |
| BEHAVIOR | |
| VOICE | |
| BODY | |
| LEGS / FEET | |
| HABITAT | |

## LOCATION

LOCATION NAME

GPS COORDINATES

— ○ ○ ○ ○ ○

— ○ ○ ○ ○ ○

## MONTH SPOTTED

| J | F | M | A | M | J | J | A | S | O | N | D |
|---|---|---|---|---|---|---|---|---|---|---|---|

## ADDITIONAL NOTES

## PHOTO / SKETCH

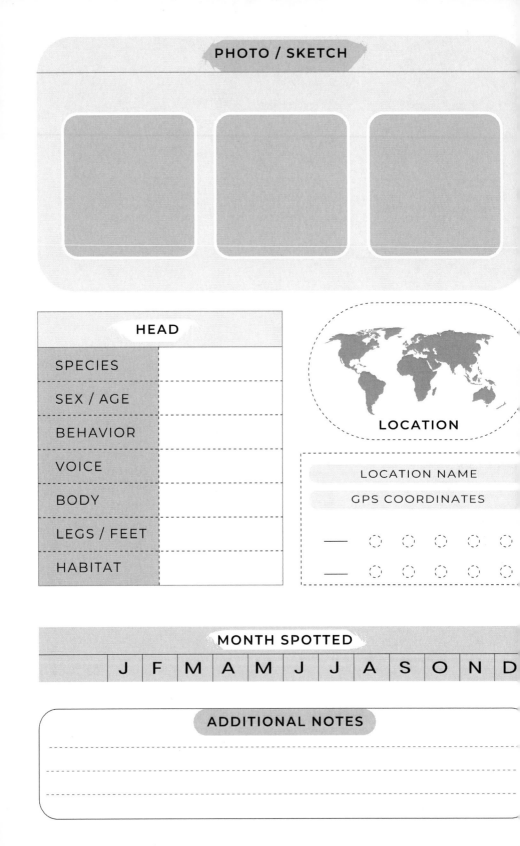

| HEAD | |
|---|---|
| SPECIES | |
| SEX / AGE | |
| BEHAVIOR | |
| VOICE | |
| BODY | |
| LEGS / FEET | |
| HABITAT | |

### LOCATION

LOCATION NAME

GPS COORDINATES

## MONTH SPOTTED

| J | F | M | A | M | J | J | A | S | O | N | D |
|---|---|---|---|---|---|---|---|---|---|---|---|

## ADDITIONAL NOTES

## HEAD

| | |
|---|---|
| SPECIES | |
| SEX / AGE | |
| BEHAVIOR | |
| VOICE | |
| BODY | |
| LEGS / FEET | |
| HABITAT | |

## LOCATION

LOCATION NAME

GPS COORDINATES

—  ◯ ◯ ◯ ◯ ◯

—  ◯ ◯ ◯ ◯ ◯

## MONTH SPOTTED

| J | F | M | A | M | J | J | A | S | O | N | D |
|---|---|---|---|---|---|---|---|---|---|---|---|

## ADDITIONAL NOTES

## PHOTO / SKETCH

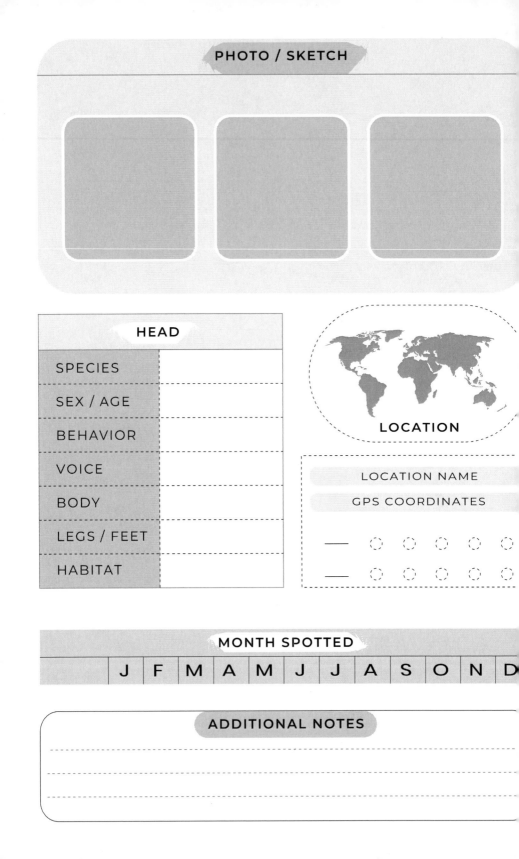

## HEAD

| | |
|---|---|
| SPECIES | |
| SEX / AGE | |
| BEHAVIOR | |
| VOICE | |
| BODY | |
| LEGS / FEET | |
| HABITAT | |

## LOCATION

LOCATION NAME

GPS COORDINATES

## MONTH SPOTTED

| J | F | M | A | M | J | J | A | S | O | N | D |
|---|---|---|---|---|---|---|---|---|---|---|---|

## ADDITIONAL NOTES

## HEAD

| SPECIES | |
|---|---|
| SEX / AGE | |
| BEHAVIOR | |
| VOICE | |
| BODY | |
| LEGS / FEET | |
| HABITAT | |

## LOCATION

LOCATION NAME

GPS COORDINATES

— ○ ○ ○ ○ ○

— ○ ○ ○ ○ ○

## MONTH SPOTTED

| J | F | M | A | M | J | J | A | S | O | N | D |
|---|---|---|---|---|---|---|---|---|---|---|---|

## ADDITIONAL NOTES

## PHOTO / SKETCH

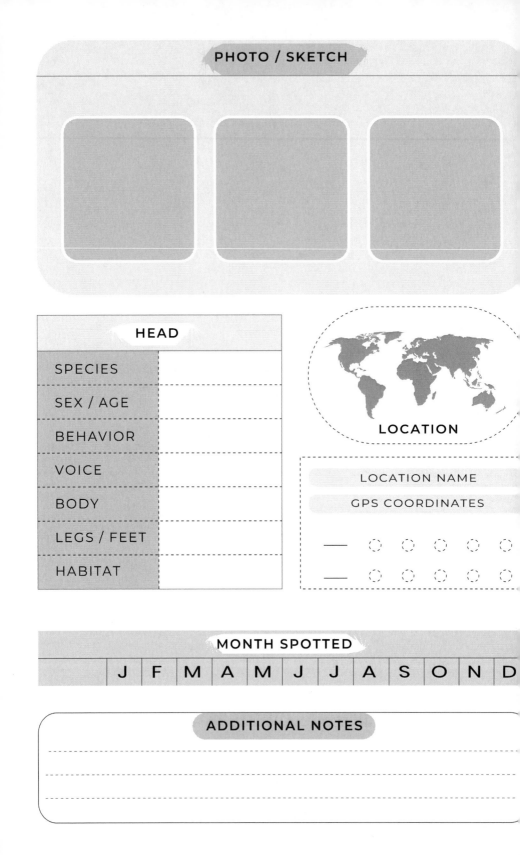

### HEAD

| | |
|---|---|
| SPECIES | |
| SEX / AGE | |
| BEHAVIOR | |
| VOICE | |
| BODY | |
| LEGS / FEET | |
| HABITAT | |

### LOCATION

LOCATION NAME

GPS COORDINATES

## MONTH SPOTTED

| J | F | M | A | M | J | J | A | S | O | N | D |
|---|---|---|---|---|---|---|---|---|---|---|---|

## ADDITIONAL NOTES

## HEAD

| | |
|---|---|
| SPECIES | |
| SEX / AGE | |
| BEHAVIOR | |
| VOICE | |
| BODY | |
| LEGS / FEET | |
| HABITAT | |

### LOCATION

LOCATION NAME

GPS COORDINATES

— ○ ○ ○ ○ ○

— ○ ○ ○ ○ ○

## MONTH SPOTTED

| J | F | M | A | M | J | J | A | S | O | N | D |
|---|---|---|---|---|---|---|---|---|---|---|---|

## ADDITIONAL NOTES

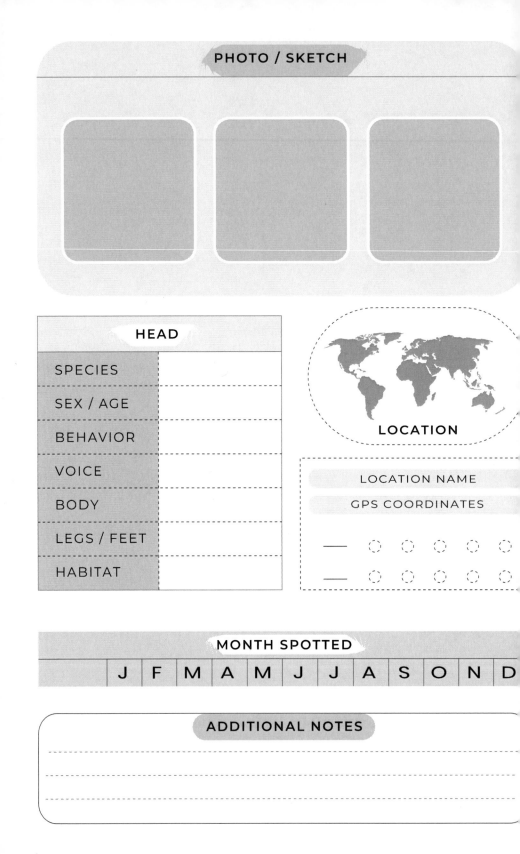

## PHOTO / SKETCH

### HEAD

| | |
|---|---|
| SPECIES | |
| SEX / AGE | |
| BEHAVIOR | |
| VOICE | |
| BODY | |
| LEGS / FEET | |
| HABITAT | |

### LOCATION

LOCATION NAME

GPS COORDINATES

### MONTH SPOTTED

| J | F | M | A | M | J | J | A | S | O | N | D |
|---|---|---|---|---|---|---|---|---|---|---|---|

### ADDITIONAL NOTES

## HEAD

| SPECIES | |
| --- | --- |
| SEX / AGE | |
| BEHAVIOR | |
| VOICE | |
| BODY | |
| LEGS / FEET | |
| HABITAT | |

## LOCATION

LOCATION NAME

GPS COORDINATES

— ○ ○ ○ ○ ○
— ○ ○ ○ ○ ○

## MONTH SPOTTED

| J | F | M | A | M | J | J | A | S | O | N | D |
| --- | --- | --- | --- | --- | --- | --- | --- | --- | --- | --- | --- |

## ADDITIONAL NOTES

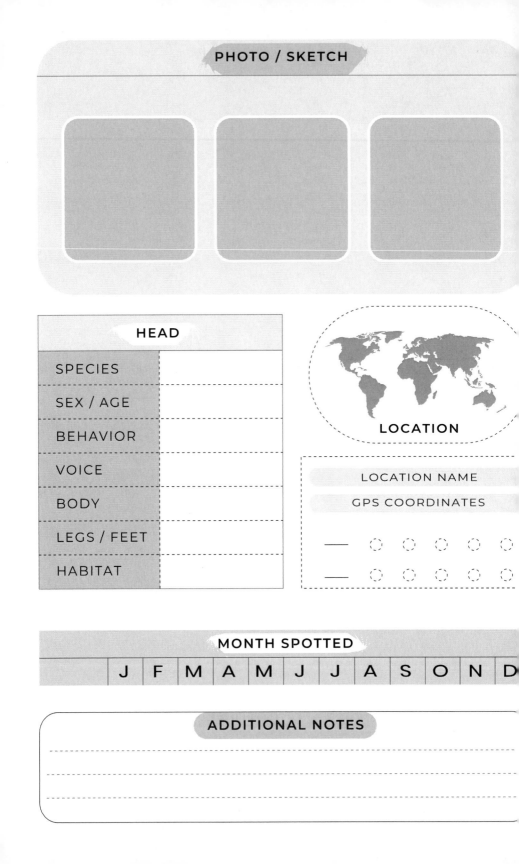

## PHOTO / SKETCH

### HEAD

| | |
|---|---|
| SPECIES | |
| SEX / AGE | |
| BEHAVIOR | |
| VOICE | |
| BODY | |
| LEGS / FEET | |
| HABITAT | |

### LOCATION

LOCATION NAME

GPS COORDINATES

## MONTH SPOTTED

| J | F | M | A | M | J | J | A | S | O | N | D |
|---|---|---|---|---|---|---|---|---|---|---|---|

## ADDITIONAL NOTES

## PHOTO / SKETCH

## HEAD

| | |
|---|---|
| SPECIES | |
| SEX / AGE | |
| BEHAVIOR | |
| VOICE | |
| BODY | |
| LEGS / FEET | |
| HABITAT | |

## LOCATION

LOCATION NAME

GPS COORDINATES

— ○ ○ ○ ○ ○

— ○ ○ ○ ○ ○

## MONTH SPOTTED

| J | F | M | A | M | J | J | A | S | O | N | D |
|---|---|---|---|---|---|---|---|---|---|---|---|

## ADDITIONAL NOTES

## PHOTO / SKETCH

### HEAD

| | |
|---|---|
| SPECIES | |
| SEX / AGE | |
| BEHAVIOR | |
| VOICE | |
| BODY | |
| LEGS / FEET | |
| HABITAT | |

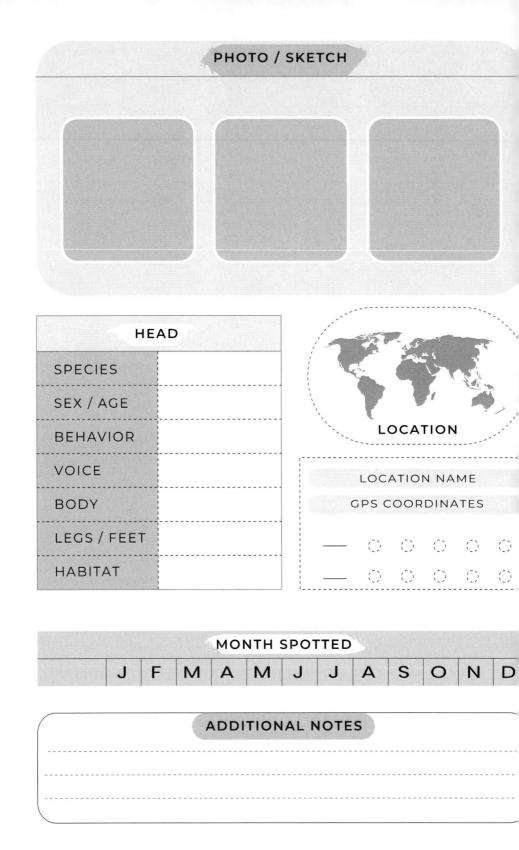

### LOCATION

LOCATION NAME

GPS COORDINATES

___ ◌ ◌ ◌ ◌ ◌

___ ◌ ◌ ◌ ◌ ◌

### MONTH SPOTTED

| J | F | M | A | M | J | J | A | S | O | N | D |
|---|---|---|---|---|---|---|---|---|---|---|---|

### ADDITIONAL NOTES

## PHOTO / SKETCH

## HEAD

| SPECIES | |
| --- | --- |
| SEX / AGE | |
| BEHAVIOR | |
| VOICE | |
| BODY | |
| LEGS / FEET | |
| HABITAT | |

## LOCATION

LOCATION NAME

GPS COORDINATES

## MONTH SPOTTED

| J | F | M | A | M | J | J | A | S | O | N | D |

## ADDITIONAL NOTES

## PHOTO / SKETCH

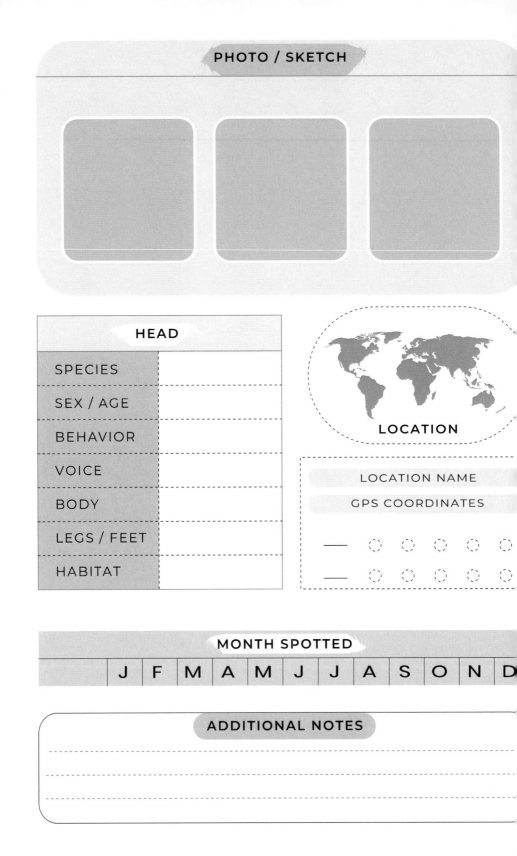

### HEAD

| | |
|---|---|
| SPECIES | |
| SEX / AGE | |
| BEHAVIOR | |
| VOICE | |
| BODY | |
| LEGS / FEET | |
| HABITAT | |

### LOCATION

LOCATION NAME

GPS COORDINATES

## MONTH SPOTTED

| J | F | M | A | M | J | J | A | S | O | N | D |
|---|---|---|---|---|---|---|---|---|---|---|---|

## ADDITIONAL NOTES

## PHOTO / SKETCH

## HEAD

| | |
|---|---|
| SPECIES | |
| SEX / AGE | |
| BEHAVIOR | |
| VOICE | |
| BODY | |
| LEGS / FEET | |
| HABITAT | |

## LOCATION

LOCATION NAME

GPS COORDINATES

___ ○ ○ ○ ○ ○

___ ○ ○ ○ ○ ○

## MONTH SPOTTED

| J | F | M | A | M | J | J | A | S | O | N | D |
|---|---|---|---|---|---|---|---|---|---|---|---|
| | | | | | | | | | | | |

## ADDITIONAL NOTES

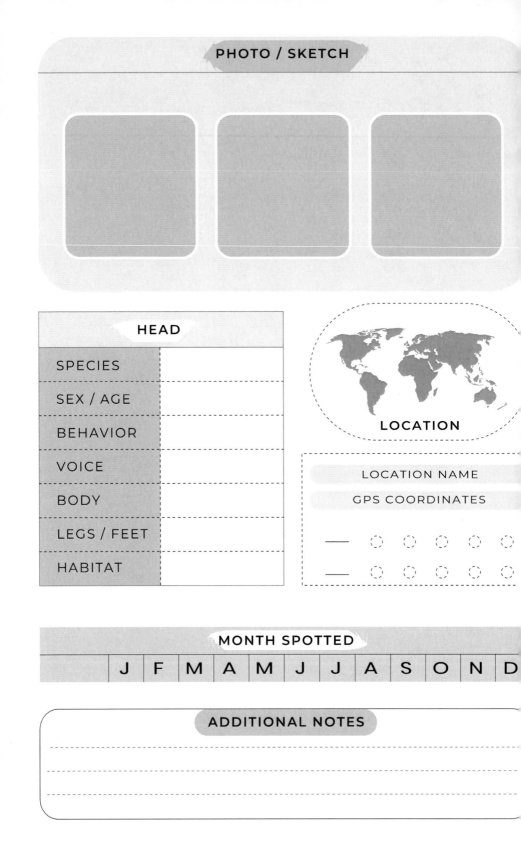

## PHOTO / SKETCH

## HEAD

| | |
|---|---|
| SPECIES | |
| SEX / AGE | |
| BEHAVIOR | |
| VOICE | |
| BODY | |
| LEGS / FEET | |
| HABITAT | |

## LOCATION

LOCATION NAME

GPS COORDINATES

## MONTH SPOTTED

| J | F | M | A | M | J | J | A | S | O | N | D |
|---|---|---|---|---|---|---|---|---|---|---|---|

## ADDITIONAL NOTES

## PHOTO / SKETCH

## HEAD

| SPECIES | |
| --- | --- |
| SEX / AGE | |
| BEHAVIOR | |
| VOICE | |
| BODY | |
| LEGS / FEET | |
| HABITAT | |

### LOCATION

LOCATION NAME

GPS COORDINATES

— ◌ ◌ ◌ ◌ ◌
— ◌ ◌ ◌ ◌ ◌

## MONTH SPOTTED

| J | F | M | A | M | J | J | A | S | O | N | D |
| --- | --- | --- | --- | --- | --- | --- | --- | --- | --- | --- | --- |

## ADDITIONAL NOTES

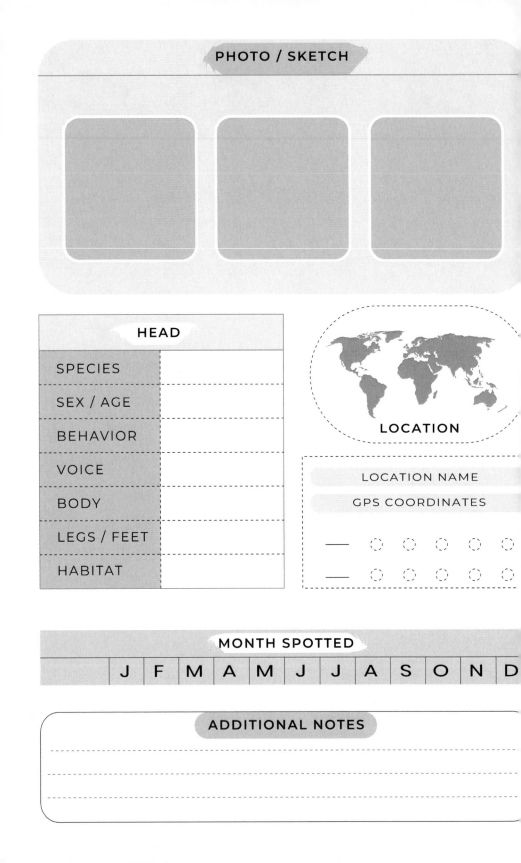

## PHOTO / SKETCH

## HEAD

| | |
|---|---|
| SPECIES | |
| SEX / AGE | |
| BEHAVIOR | |
| VOICE | |
| BODY | |
| LEGS / FEET | |
| HABITAT | |

## LOCATION

LOCATION NAME

GPS COORDINATES

## MONTH SPOTTED

| J | F | M | A | M | J | J | A | S | O | N | D |
|---|---|---|---|---|---|---|---|---|---|---|---|

## ADDITIONAL NOTES

## PHOTO / SKETCH

## HEAD

| SPECIES | |
|---|---|
| SEX / AGE | |
| BEHAVIOR | |
| VOICE | |
| BODY | |
| LEGS / FEET | |
| HABITAT | |

## LOCATION

LOCATION NAME

GPS COORDINATES

## MONTH SPOTTED

| J | F | M | A | M | J | J | A | S | O | N | D |
|---|---|---|---|---|---|---|---|---|---|---|---|

## ADDITIONAL NOTES

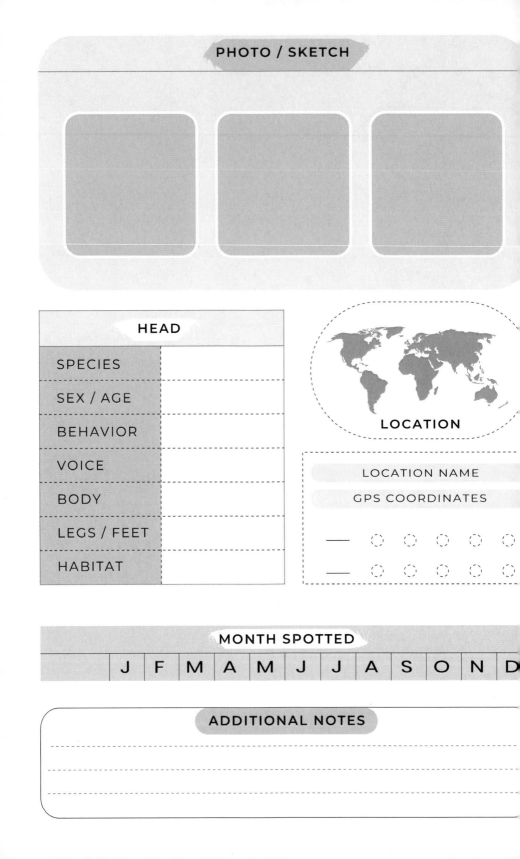

## PHOTO / SKETCH

### HEAD

| | |
|---|---|
| SPECIES | |
| SEX / AGE | |
| BEHAVIOR | |
| VOICE | |
| BODY | |
| LEGS / FEET | |
| HABITAT | |

### LOCATION

LOCATION NAME

GPS COORDINATES

## MONTH SPOTTED

| J | F | M | A | M | J | J | A | S | O | N | D |
|---|---|---|---|---|---|---|---|---|---|---|---|

## ADDITIONAL NOTES

## PHOTO / SKETCH

### HEAD

| | |
|---|---|
| SPECIES | |
| SEX / AGE | |
| BEHAVIOR | |
| VOICE | |
| BODY | |
| LEGS / FEET | |
| HABITAT | |

### LOCATION

LOCATION NAME

GPS COORDINATES

— ○ ○ ○ ○ ○
— ○ ○ ○ ○ ○

### MONTH SPOTTED

| J | F | M | A | M | J | J | A | S | O | N | D |
|---|---|---|---|---|---|---|---|---|---|---|---|

### ADDITIONAL NOTES

# PHOTO / SKETCH

## HEAD

| | |
|---|---|
| SPECIES | |
| SEX / AGE | |
| BEHAVIOR | |
| VOICE | |
| BODY | |
| LEGS / FEET | |
| HABITAT | |

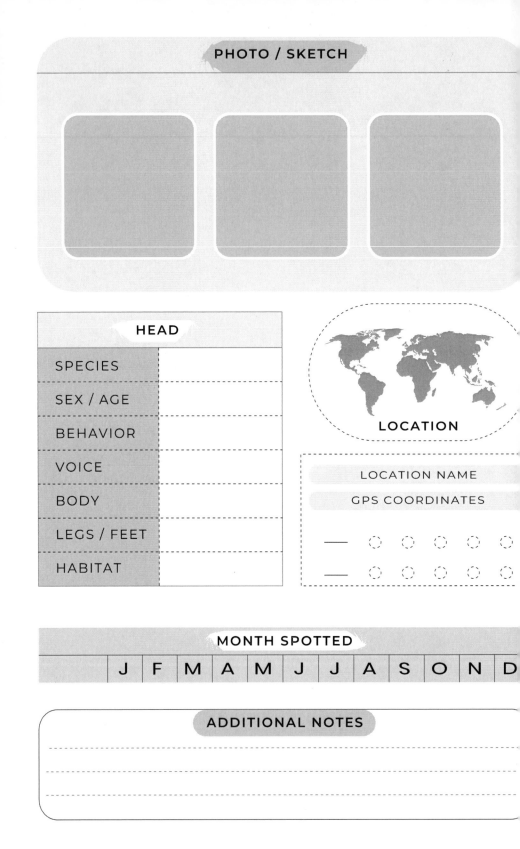

## LOCATION

LOCATION NAME

GPS COORDINATES

— ○ ○ ○ ○ ○

— ○ ○ ○ ○ ○

## MONTH SPOTTED

| J | F | M | A | M | J | J | A | S | O | N | D |
|---|---|---|---|---|---|---|---|---|---|---|---|

## ADDITIONAL NOTES

## PHOTO / SKETCH

## HEAD

| SPECIES | |
| --- | --- |
| SEX / AGE | |
| BEHAVIOR | |
| VOICE | |
| BODY | |
| LEGS / FEET | |
| HABITAT | |

## LOCATION

LOCATION NAME

GPS COORDINATES

___ ○ ○ ○ ○ ○

___ ○ ○ ○ ○ ○

## MONTH SPOTTED

| J | F | M | A | M | J | J | A | S | O | N | D |
| --- | --- | --- | --- | --- | --- | --- | --- | --- | --- | --- | --- |

## ADDITIONAL NOTES

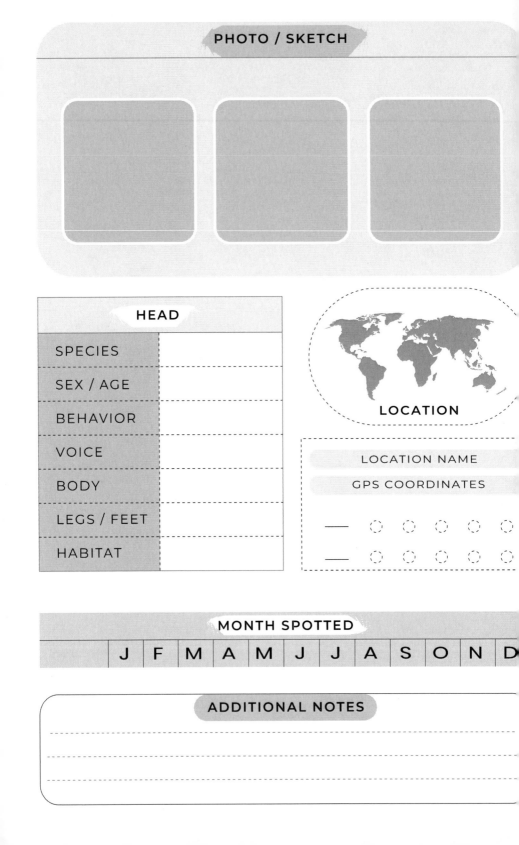

## PHOTO / SKETCH

## HEAD

| | |
|---|---|
| SPECIES | |
| SEX / AGE | |
| BEHAVIOR | |
| VOICE | |
| BODY | |
| LEGS / FEET | |
| HABITAT | |

## LOCATION

LOCATION NAME

GPS COORDINATES

## MONTH SPOTTED

| J | F | M | A | M | J | J | A | S | O | N | D |
|---|---|---|---|---|---|---|---|---|---|---|---|

## ADDITIONAL NOTES

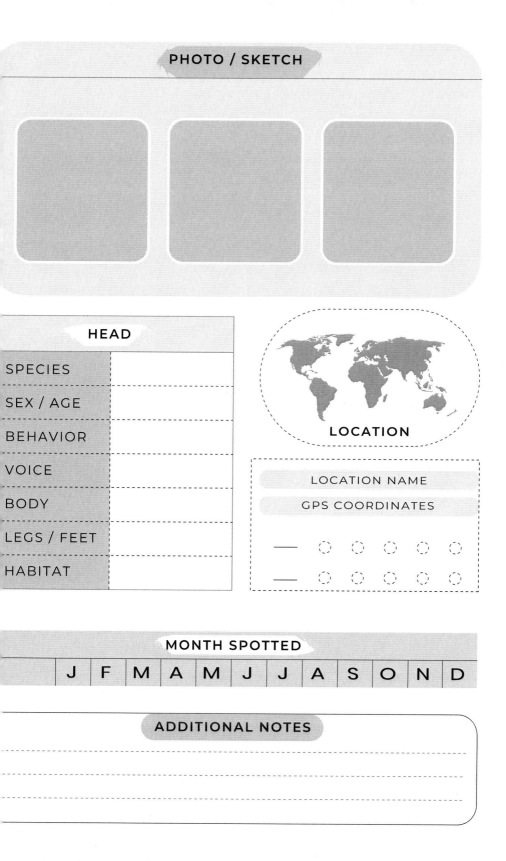

## PHOTO / SKETCH

### HEAD

| SPECIES | |
| --- | --- |
| SEX / AGE | |
| BEHAVIOR | |
| VOICE | |
| BODY | |
| LEGS / FEET | |
| HABITAT | |

### LOCATION

LOCATION NAME

GPS COORDINATES

## MONTH SPOTTED

| J | F | M | A | M | J | J | A | S | O | N | D |

## ADDITIONAL NOTES

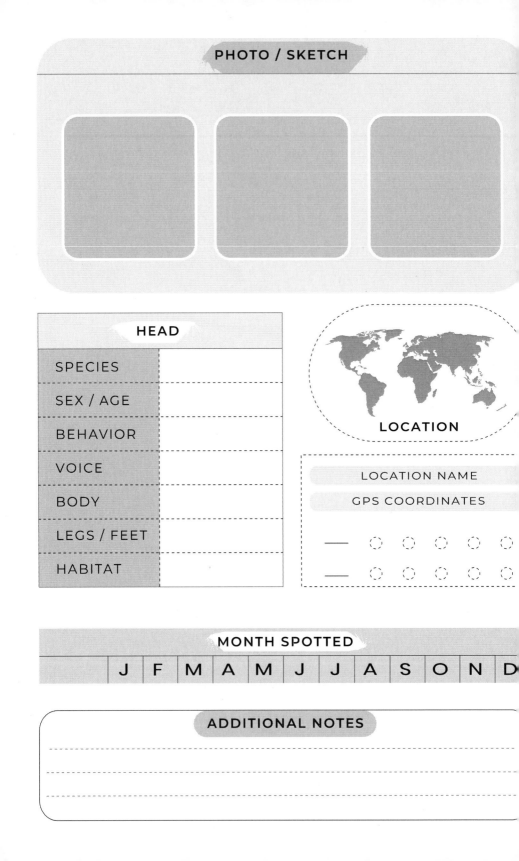

## PHOTO / SKETCH

## HEAD

| | |
|---|---|
| SPECIES | |
| SEX / AGE | |
| BEHAVIOR | |
| VOICE | |
| BODY | |
| LEGS / FEET | |
| HABITAT | |

## LOCATION

LOCATION NAME

GPS COORDINATES

## MONTH SPOTTED

| J | F | M | A | M | J | J | A | S | O | N | D |
|---|---|---|---|---|---|---|---|---|---|---|---|

## ADDITIONAL NOTES

## PHOTO / SKETCH

## HEAD

| | |
|---|---|
| SPECIES | |
| SEX / AGE | |
| BEHAVIOR | |
| VOICE | |
| BODY | |
| LEGS / FEET | |
| HABITAT | |

## LOCATION

LOCATION NAME

GPS COORDINATES

## MONTH SPOTTED

| J | F | M | A | M | J | J | A | S | O | N | D |
|---|---|---|---|---|---|---|---|---|---|---|---|

## ADDITIONAL NOTES

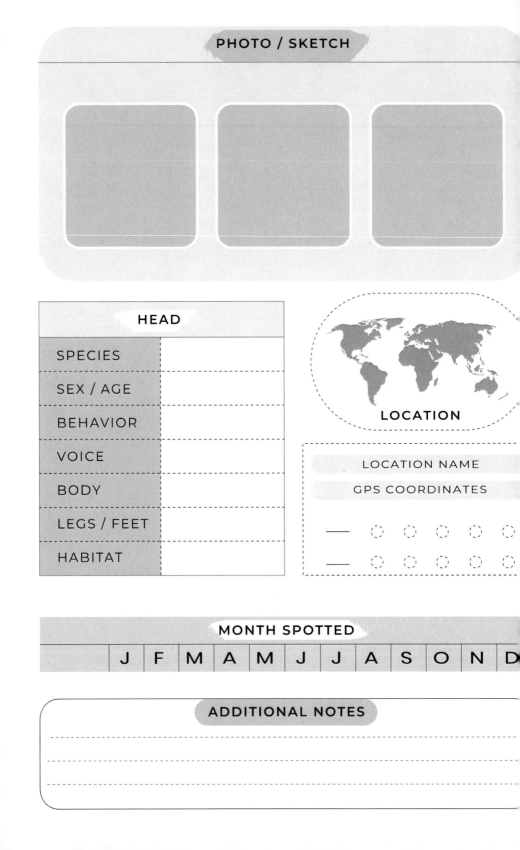

## PHOTO / SKETCH

### HEAD

| | |
|---|---|
| SPECIES | |
| SEX / AGE | |
| BEHAVIOR | |
| VOICE | |
| BODY | |
| LEGS / FEET | |
| HABITAT | |

### LOCATION

LOCATION NAME

GPS COORDINATES

### MONTH SPOTTED

| J | F | M | A | M | J | J | A | S | O | N | D |

### ADDITIONAL NOTES

## PHOTO / SKETCH

## HEAD

| | |
|---|---|
| SPECIES | |
| SEX / AGE | |
| BEHAVIOR | |
| VOICE | |
| BODY | |
| LEGS / FEET | |
| HABITAT | |

## LOCATION

LOCATION NAME

GPS COORDINATES

## MONTH SPOTTED

| J | F | M | A | M | J | J | A | S | O | N | D |

## ADDITIONAL NOTES

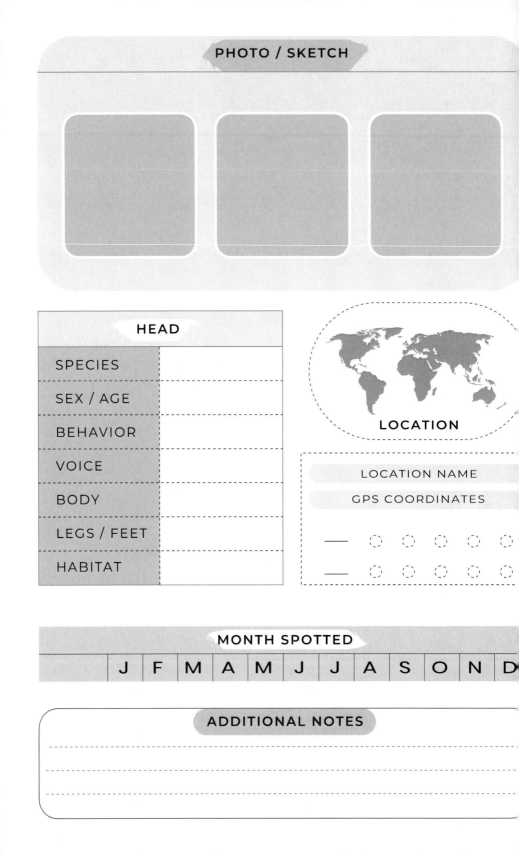

## PHOTO / SKETCH

### HEAD

| | |
|---|---|
| SPECIES | |
| SEX / AGE | |
| BEHAVIOR | |
| VOICE | |
| BODY | |
| LEGS / FEET | |
| HABITAT | |

### LOCATION

LOCATION NAME

GPS COORDINATES

### MONTH SPOTTED

| J | F | M | A | M | J | J | A | S | O | N | D |
|---|---|---|---|---|---|---|---|---|---|---|---|

### ADDITIONAL NOTES

## PHOTO / SKETCH

## HEAD

| | |
|---|---|
| SPECIES | |
| SEX / AGE | |
| BEHAVIOR | |
| VOICE | |
| BODY | |
| LEGS / FEET | |
| HABITAT | |

## LOCATION

LOCATION NAME

GPS COORDINATES

— ◯ ◯ ◯ ◯ ◯
— ◯ ◯ ◯ ◯ ◯

## MONTH SPOTTED

| J | F | M | A | M | J | J | A | S | O | N | D |
|---|---|---|---|---|---|---|---|---|---|---|---|

## ADDITIONAL NOTES

## PHOTO / SKETCH

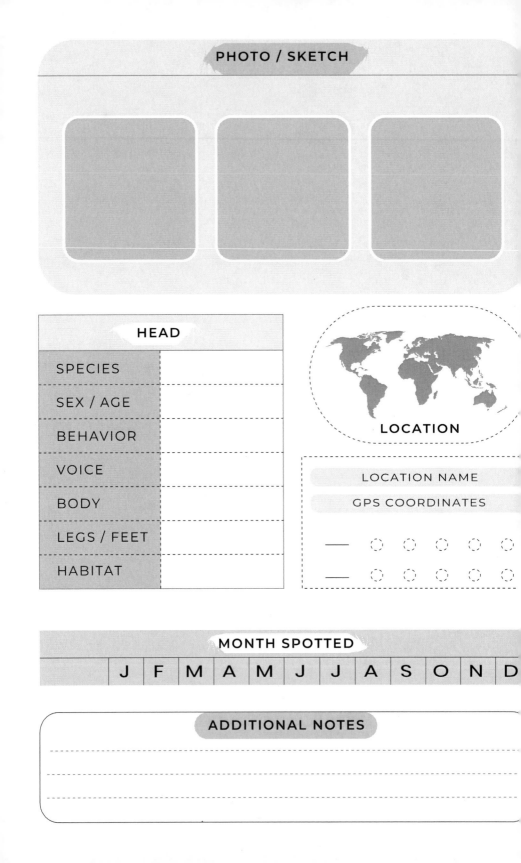

### HEAD

| | |
|---|---|
| SPECIES | |
| SEX / AGE | |
| BEHAVIOR | |
| VOICE | |
| BODY | |
| LEGS / FEET | |
| HABITAT | |

### LOCATION

LOCATION NAME

GPS COORDINATES

## MONTH SPOTTED

| J | F | M | A | M | J | J | A | S | O | N | D |
|---|---|---|---|---|---|---|---|---|---|---|---|

## ADDITIONAL NOTES

## PHOTO / SKETCH

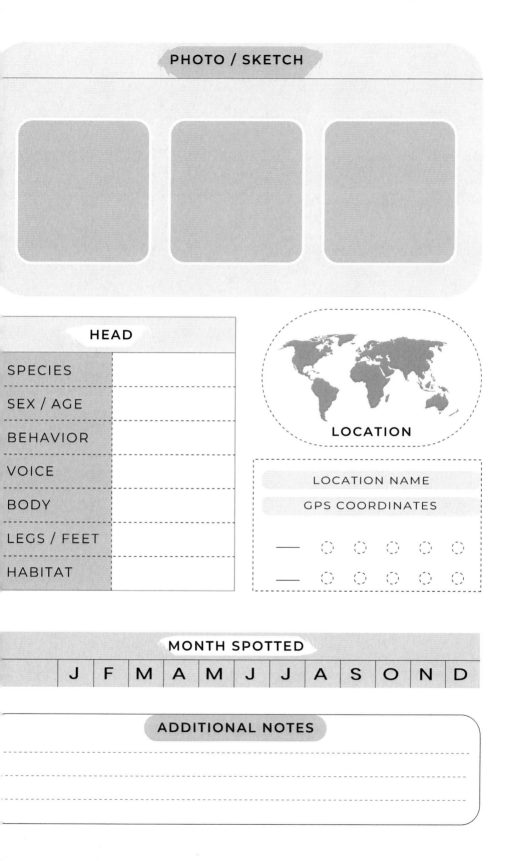

## HEAD

| | |
|---|---|
| SPECIES | |
| SEX / AGE | |
| BEHAVIOR | |
| VOICE | |
| BODY | |
| LEGS / FEET | |
| HABITAT | |

## LOCATION

LOCATION NAME

GPS COORDINATES

## MONTH SPOTTED

| J | F | M | A | M | J | J | A | S | O | N | D |
|---|---|---|---|---|---|---|---|---|---|---|---|

## ADDITIONAL NOTES

## PHOTO / SKETCH

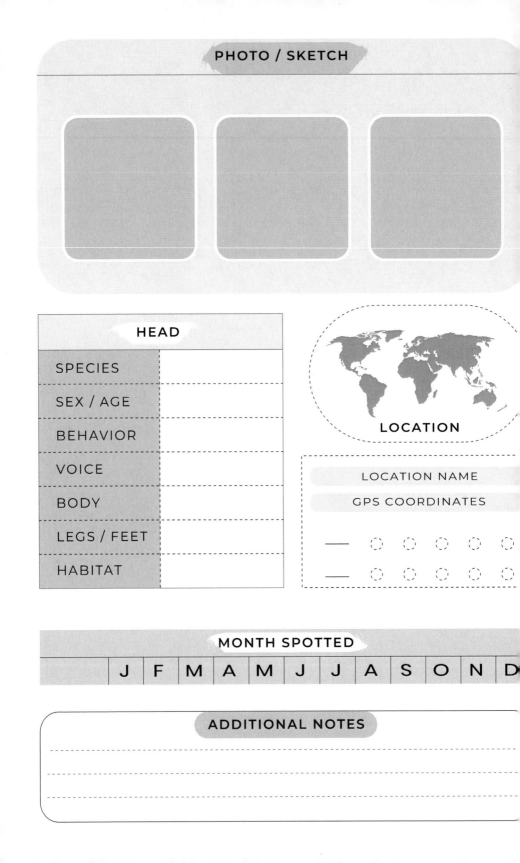

### HEAD

| | |
|---|---|
| SPECIES | |
| SEX / AGE | |
| BEHAVIOR | |
| VOICE | |
| BODY | |
| LEGS / FEET | |
| HABITAT | |

### LOCATION

LOCATION NAME

GPS COORDINATES

### MONTH SPOTTED

| J | F | M | A | M | J | J | A | S | O | N | D |
|---|---|---|---|---|---|---|---|---|---|---|---|

### ADDITIONAL NOTES

## PHOTO / SKETCH

## HEAD

| SPECIES | |
| --- | --- |
| SEX / AGE | |
| BEHAVIOR | |
| VOICE | |
| BODY | |
| LEGS / FEET | |
| HABITAT | |

### LOCATION

LOCATION NAME

GPS COORDINATES

## MONTH SPOTTED

| J | F | M | A | M | J | J | A | S | O | N | D |

## ADDITIONAL NOTES

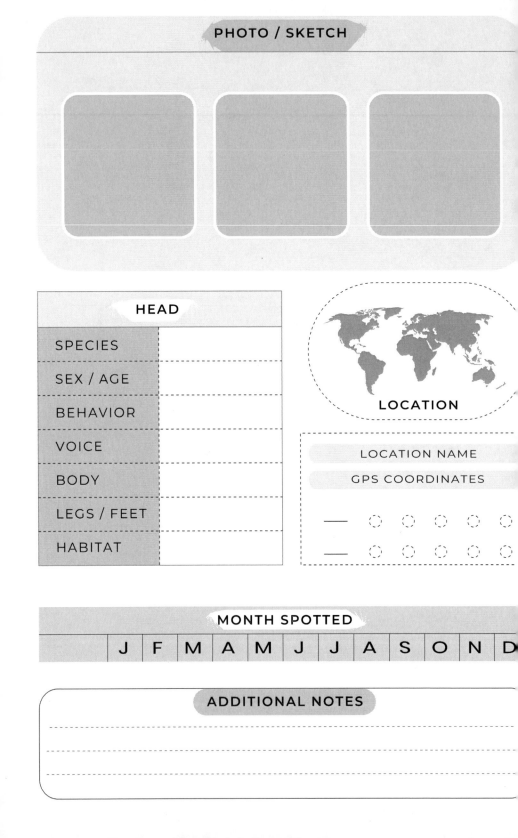

## PHOTO / SKETCH

### HEAD

| | |
|---|---|
| SPECIES | |
| SEX / AGE | |
| BEHAVIOR | |
| VOICE | |
| BODY | |
| LEGS / FEET | |
| HABITAT | |

### LOCATION

LOCATION NAME

GPS COORDINATES

### MONTH SPOTTED

| J | F | M | A | M | J | J | A | S | O | N | D |
|---|---|---|---|---|---|---|---|---|---|---|---|

### ADDITIONAL NOTES

## PHOTO / SKETCH

## HEAD

| | |
|---|---|
| SPECIES | |
| SEX / AGE | |
| BEHAVIOR | |
| VOICE | |
| BODY | |
| LEGS / FEET | |
| HABITAT | |

## LOCATION

LOCATION NAME

GPS COORDINATES

—  ○ ○ ○ ○ ○
—  ○ ○ ○ ○ ○

## MONTH SPOTTED

| J | F | M | A | M | J | J | A | S | O | N | D |
|---|---|---|---|---|---|---|---|---|---|---|---|

## ADDITIONAL NOTES

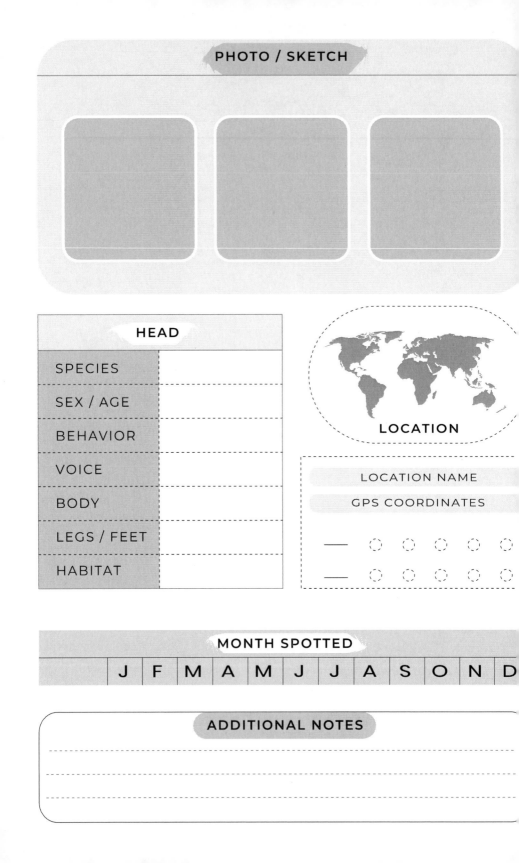

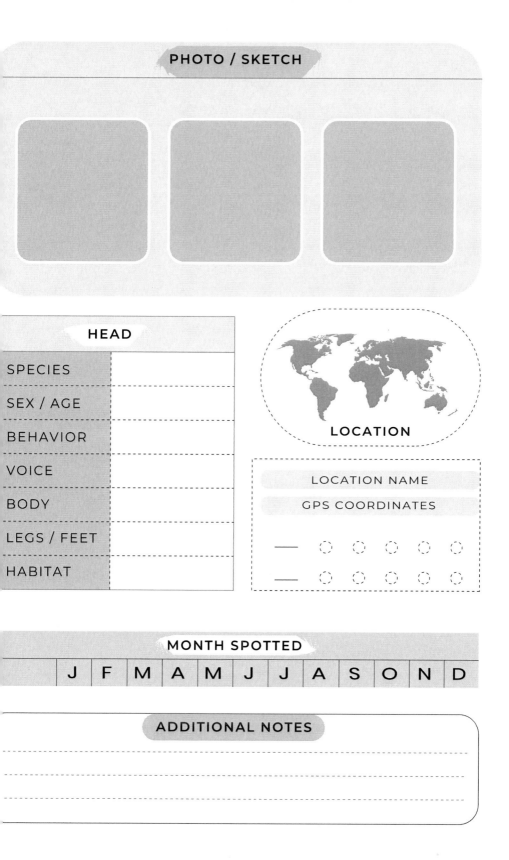

## PHOTO / SKETCH

## HEAD

| | |
|---|---|
| SPECIES | |
| SEX / AGE | |
| BEHAVIOR | |
| VOICE | |
| BODY | |
| LEGS / FEET | |
| HABITAT | |

## LOCATION

LOCATION NAME

GPS COORDINATES

## MONTH SPOTTED

| J | F | M | A | M | J | J | A | S | O | N | D |

## ADDITIONAL NOTES

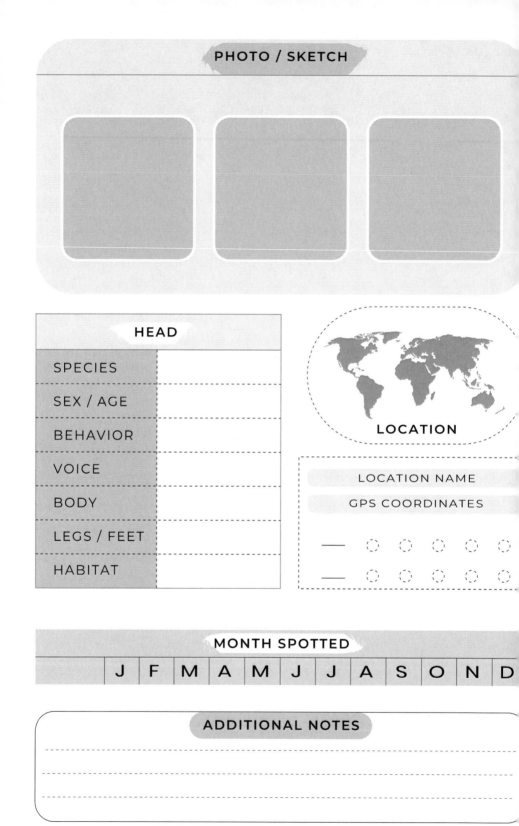

## PHOTO / SKETCH

## HEAD

| | |
|---|---|
| SPECIES | |
| SEX / AGE | |
| BEHAVIOR | |
| VOICE | |
| BODY | |
| LEGS / FEET | |
| HABITAT | |

## LOCATION

LOCATION NAME

GPS COORDINATES

## MONTH SPOTTED

| J | F | M | A | M | J | J | A | S | O | N | D |
|---|---|---|---|---|---|---|---|---|---|---|---|

## ADDITIONAL NOTES

## PHOTO / SKETCH

## HEAD

| | |
|---|---|
| SPECIES | |
| SEX / AGE | |
| BEHAVIOR | |
| VOICE | |
| BODY | |
| LEGS / FEET | |
| HABITAT | |

## LOCATION

LOCATION NAME

GPS COORDINATES

— ○ ○ ○ ○ ○

— ○ ○ ○ ○ ○

## MONTH SPOTTED

| J | F | M | A | M | J | J | A | S | O | N | D |
|---|---|---|---|---|---|---|---|---|---|---|---|

## ADDITIONAL NOTES

# PHOTO / SKETCH

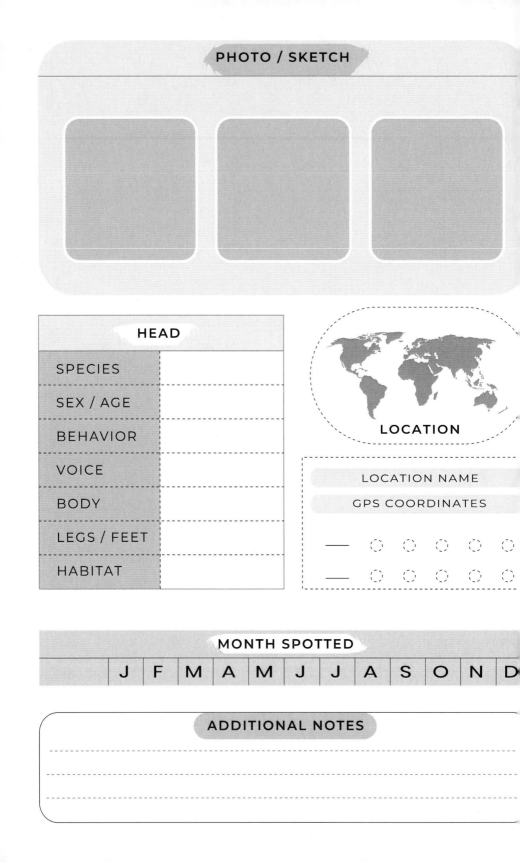

## HEAD

| | |
|---|---|
| SPECIES | |
| SEX / AGE | |
| BEHAVIOR | |
| VOICE | |
| BODY | |
| LEGS / FEET | |
| HABITAT | |

## LOCATION

LOCATION NAME

GPS COORDINATES

## MONTH SPOTTED

| J | F | M | A | M | J | J | A | S | O | N | D |
|---|---|---|---|---|---|---|---|---|---|---|---|

## ADDITIONAL NOTES

## HEAD

| SPECIES | |
|---|---|
| SEX / AGE | |
| BEHAVIOR | |
| VOICE | |
| BODY | |
| LEGS / FEET | |
| HABITAT | |

## LOCATION

LOCATION NAME

GPS COORDINATES

— ○ ○ ○ ○ ○

— ○ ○ ○ ○ ○

## MONTH SPOTTED

| J | F | M | A | M | J | J | A | S | O | N | D |
|---|---|---|---|---|---|---|---|---|---|---|---|

## ADDITIONAL NOTES

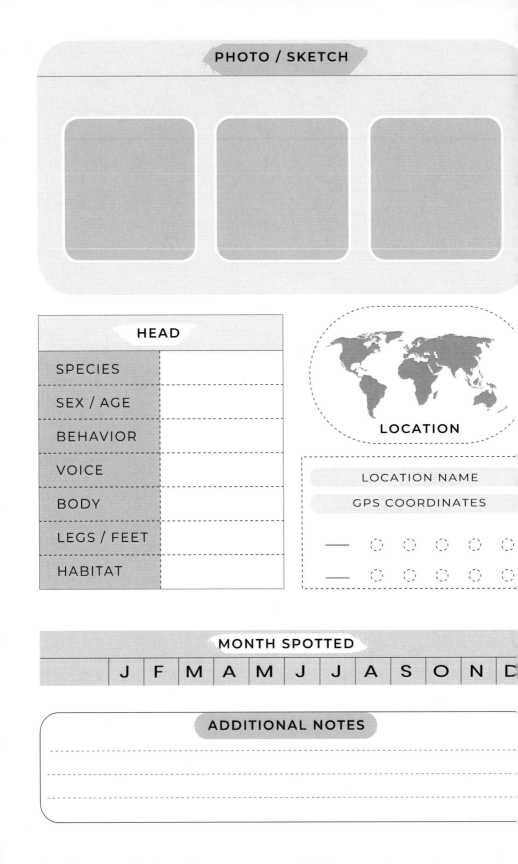

## PHOTO / SKETCH

## HEAD

| | |
|---|---|
| SPECIES | |
| SEX / AGE | |
| BEHAVIOR | |
| VOICE | |
| BODY | |
| LEGS / FEET | |
| HABITAT | |

## LOCATION

LOCATION NAME

GPS COORDINATES

## MONTH SPOTTED

| J | F | M | A | M | J | J | A | S | O | N | D |
|---|---|---|---|---|---|---|---|---|---|---|---|

## ADDITIONAL NOTES

## PHOTO / SKETCH

## HEAD

| SPECIES | |
|---|---|
| SEX / AGE | |
| BEHAVIOR | |
| VOICE | |
| BODY | |
| LEGS / FEET | |
| HABITAT | |

## LOCATION

LOCATION NAME

GPS COORDINATES

— ⊙ ⊙ ⊙ ⊙ ⊙

— ⊙ ⊙ ⊙ ⊙ ⊙

## MONTH SPOTTED

| J | F | M | A | M | J | J | A | S | O | N | D |
|---|---|---|---|---|---|---|---|---|---|---|---|

## ADDITIONAL NOTES

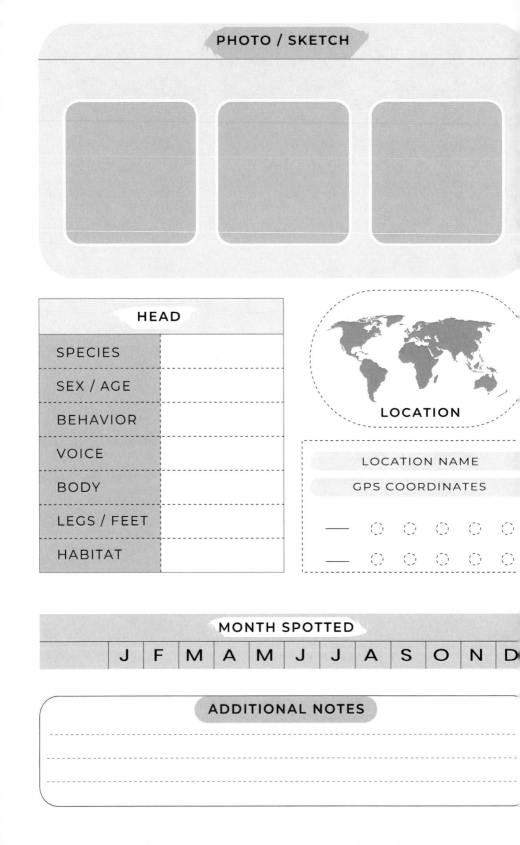

## PHOTO / SKETCH

### HEAD

| | |
|---|---|
| SPECIES | |
| SEX / AGE | |
| BEHAVIOR | |
| VOICE | |
| BODY | |
| LEGS / FEET | |
| HABITAT | |

### LOCATION

LOCATION NAME

GPS COORDINATES

## MONTH SPOTTED

| J | F | M | A | M | J | J | A | S | O | N | D |
|---|---|---|---|---|---|---|---|---|---|---|---|

## ADDITIONAL NOTES

Made in United States
North Haven, CT
30 April 2022

18757501R00067